WORLD OF KNOWLEDGE

Early Civilizations

Ron Carter

Macdonald/Silver Burdett

Editorial Manager	Chester Fisher
Senior Editor	Lynne Sabel
Editor	John Rowlstone
Assistant Editor	Bridget Daly
Series Designers	QED (Alastair Campbell and Edward Kinsey)
Designers	Jim Marks
	Nigel Osborne
Series Consultant	Keith Lye
Consultant	Peter Clayton
Production	Penny Kitchenham
Picture Research	Jenny de Gex

© Macdonald Educational Ltd. 1978
First published 1978
Reprinted 1979
Macdonald Educational Ltd.
Holywell House
Worship Street
London EC2A 2EN

Published in the
United States by
Silver Burdett Company
Morristown, N.J.
1980 Printing
ISBN 0-382-06407-0

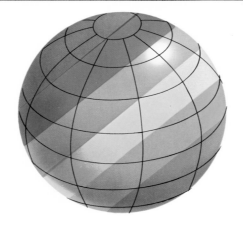

World of Knowledge

This book breaks new ground in the method it uses to present information to the reader. The unique page design combines narrative with an alphabetical reference section and it uses colourful photographs, diagrams and illustrations to provide an instant and detailed understanding of the book's theme. The main body of information is presented in a series of chapters that cover, in depth, the subject of this book. At the bottom of each page is a reference section which gives, in alphabetical order, concise articles which define, or enlarge on, the topics discussed in the chapter. Throughout the book, the use of SMALL CAPITALS in the text directs the reader to further information that is printed in the reference section. The same method is used to cross-reference entries within each reference section. Finally, there is a comprehensive index at the end of the book that will help the reader find information in the text, illustrations and reference sections. The quality of the text, and the originality of its presentation, ensure that this book can be read both for enjoyment and for the most up-to-date information on the subject.

Contents

Introduction

Early Civilizations covers a broad timespan of human history, from the emergence of early man to the creation of great civilizations in Mesopotamia, around the Mediterranean Sea and, farther afield, in eastern Asia. Early history involves dramatic accounts of the rise and fall of warring nations led by powerful kings and brilliant generals, and also of tremendous breakthroughs in science and technology, art and architecture, and philosophy and religion. But, of equal importance, there is the story of how ordinary people lived, worked and worshipped and how they were affected by new ideas and inventions. One of the most exciting aspects involved in the study of ancient history is that archaeologists are forever digging up new evidence about the distant past and **Early Civilizations** reflects the latest knowledge and the most recent theories about the origins of our cultural heritage.

4

No-one**No-one can say exactly what constitutes a civilization, nor can one say exactly when a civilization emerged or declined. Here, the historical pattern of 32 peoples shows the already complex world that had evolved by AD 1600.**

Timechart

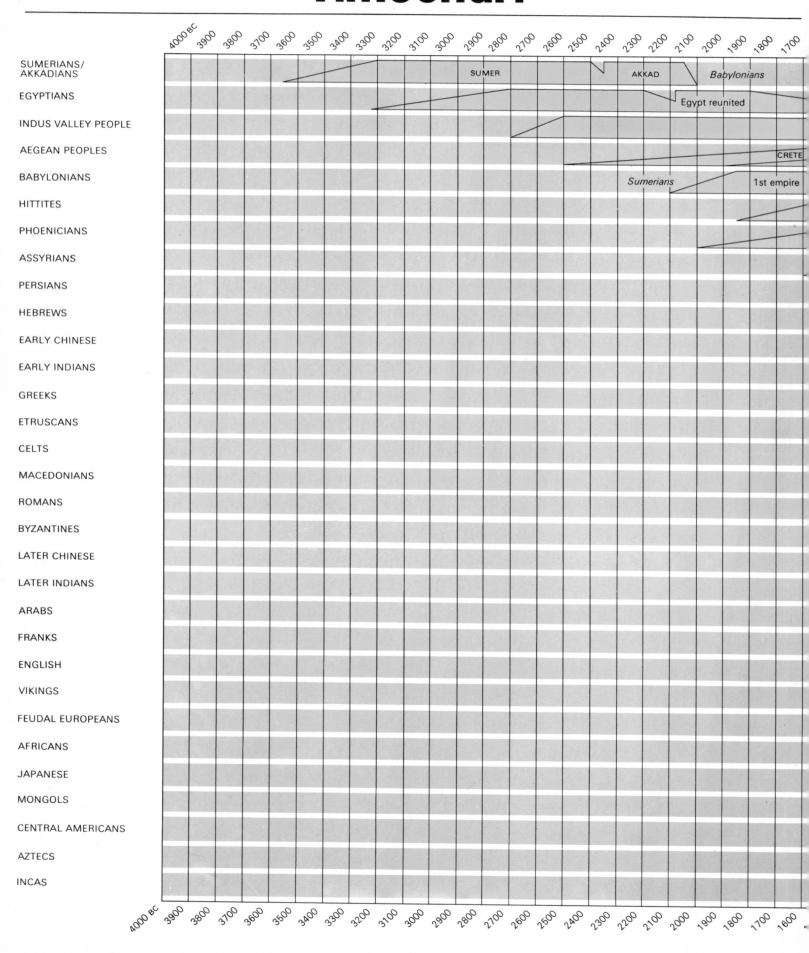

Below: This chart shows when the world's civilizations emerged, flourished and declined. All of them developed over a long period before reaching their peaks and each civilization was unique. Some declined and disappeared slowly, like the Aegean and the Byzantine. Others, like the Assyrian and the Aztec, ended abruptly following military disaster. Some civilizations owed much to earlier, barely-known predecessors. For example, the Maya owed much to the Olmecs and the Babylonians inherited their civilization from the Sumerians. Some civilizations flourished again after long decline. These included the Egyptian, Babylonian, Chinese and Indian, which all survived foreign domination. Some early civilizations, including the Hebrew, Arab, French and Japanese have, in different ways, continued into present times. The Hebrew civilization was tiny; the Mongol vast. Persia, Han China and Rome were roughly comparable. The Inca civilization lasted 2 generations; the Egyptian, over 100. (Italics are used to show connections with earlier or later civilizations.)

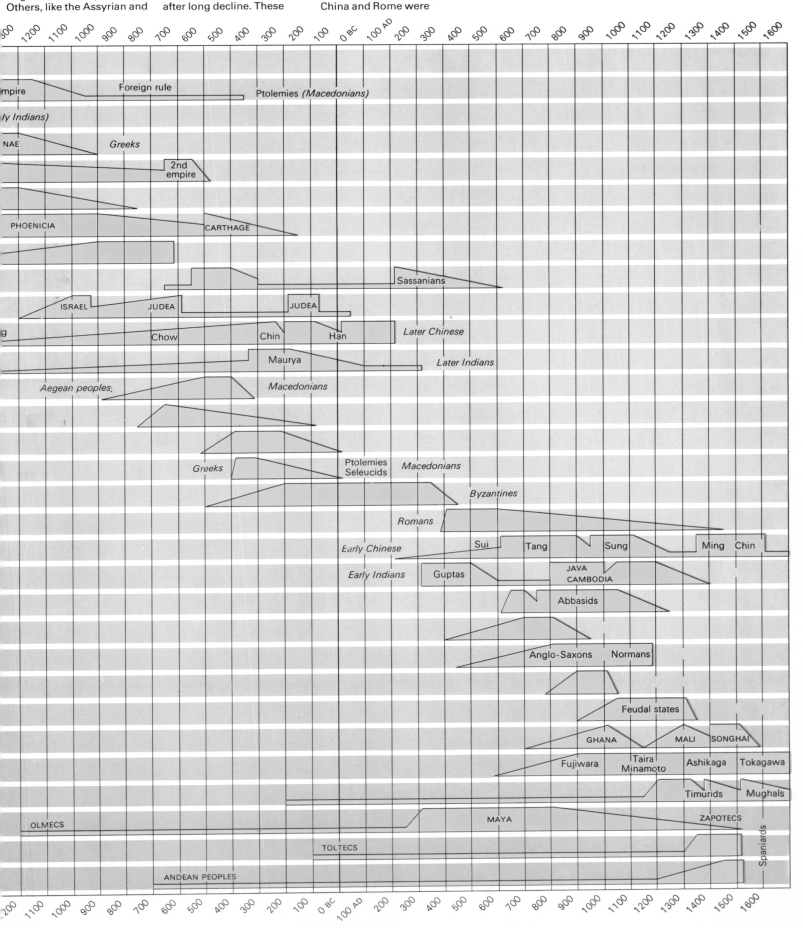

Our knowledge of the life-style and technology of early man has been pieced together by the work of archaeologists and anthropologists. New discoveries are being made all the time, filling in more pieces of the jigsaw puzzle.

Early Man

No one knows when the first true men appeared on earth. A remote ancestor of man (*Ramapithecus*) who lived in India some 14 million years ago, used sticks and stones as simple weapons. About five million years ago, man-like ape, known as AUSTRALOPITHECUS, lived in south and east Africa.

Early men

Between two and three million years ago, two types of upright, walking men, *1470 man* and *Ethiopian man*, lived in EAST AFRICA and had more advanced brains than those of any known previous species. They chipped flakes off stones to make sharp cutting edges and the Stone Age culture that they began, dominated the world until a few thousand years ago. Some scientists think they may have been our direct ancestors, but we have no certain knowledge of who our ancestors were, and we cannot be sure that all present-day men are descended from common ancestors.

Several other kinds of men lived nearer our own times. *Homo erectus* (Upright man) used fire and hunted animals over large areas of Africa, Europe and Asia perhaps 500,000 years ago. Physically, he probably had the power of speech, but we can never know to what extent he used it. *Homo sapiens* (Wise man), who lived in Denmark, Germany and England about 250,000 years ago, had a skull similar to ours in shape. One of several varieties of *Homo sapiens*, NEANDERTHAL MAN, dominated Europe 30,000 to 70,000 years ago (between the last two Ice Ages).

About 35,000 years ago, *Homo sapiens sapiens* (our own sub-species), had firmly established himself. One of his groups, CRO-MAGNON man, migrated from south-eastern Asia into France, Italy and north Africa, where he survived until 10,000 years ago. We do not know whether these early peoples mated outside their own sub-species or groups. Nor do we know why they did

Below: Stone Age man survived by adapting to his environment and making use of the materials to hand. *Left*, a boy helps his father to chip flints into tools. *Centre*, 2 men shape tree branches into spears. *Right*, 3 men take to the water on a raft. *Right*, a man prepares antlers and tusks for future use. Expertly-made axes lie in front of him. Simple tents give protection against the cold night.

not survive. Climatic change, conflict between rival groups, or changes in the available food supply may all in turn have contributed to their doom.

Through evolution, our own sub-species seems to have divided into three main 'RACES': Caucasoids, Mongoloids and Negroids. Examples from each group are: Europeans and Indians; Chinese and Japanese; and Africans. However, most of the world's peoples are mixtures of these 'races'.

Reference

A **Aborigines of Australia** provide an interesting example of Stone Age people observed by man in the AD 1800s. They probably migrated from south-eastern Asia into Australia over 30,000 years ago, before the sea covered the land bridging New Guinea to Australia. When the British landed in Australia in 1788, the Aborigines numbered about 300,000. Yet they comprised more than 5,000 tribes

speaking 300 different languages. Men used spears, harpoons, hooks, traps, nets, clubs and boomerangs to hunt animals and catch fish. They also smoked out animals and, like the ancient Americans, caught fish by drugging them with the juices of certain leaves and roots. Women and children collected roots, fruits, edible insects and honey. The Aborigines used stone and plant and animal materials skilfully. They carried firesticks and other tools in *dilly bags* woven from human hair, grasses and bark fibres.

In hunting, they often disguised themselves or covered their bodies with mud to hide their smell from their prey. They wrapped babies in tree bark for warmth, and rubbed their own bodies with animal fats against the cold. Their art portrayed myths and legends and geometrical designs. Stylized dances imitated the movements of a tribe's totem animal or bird. Their musical instruments included DIDGERIDOOS AND BULL-ROARERS. Their religion included the belief in a DREAM-TIME. The Aborigines' relig-

ion involved complex rituals, ceremonies and magic. Their witch doctors treated physical and mental illnesses skilfully.

Spanish cave paintings

Animals of importance to men 15,000 years ago included reindeer, mammoths, horses and bison. CRO-MAGNON men drew pictures of mammoths on the walls of caves in France.

Art may have begun when men scratched or painted over shadows on cave walls. The first artists then found that they could represent 3-dimensional animals and objects 2-dimensionally. This new ability gave scope to record ideas or preserve pictorially what they saw. Some of the earliest-known animal pictures were en-

Basic necessities of life

Early men gathered fruits, nuts, berries and other edible plant products. They also trapped fish and animals, devising increasingly cunning ways of doing so. They made simple WEAPONS and developed tactics to outwit their prey. About 400,000 years ago they found, probably by accident, that fire, if controlled, could be used to cook meat and other food. Control of fire gave man an even greater advantage over hostile animals.

Early man frequently migrated in the hope of finding suitable land, but whatever the conditions, he always needed to protect himself against bad weather, contrasting temperatures between day and night, and seasonal extremes. CLOTHES and shelter became increasingly complex, where holes in the ground or caves were not always available or suitable. Where possible, men made simple tents from branches and skins, or more durable structures of wood or stone. Walls or

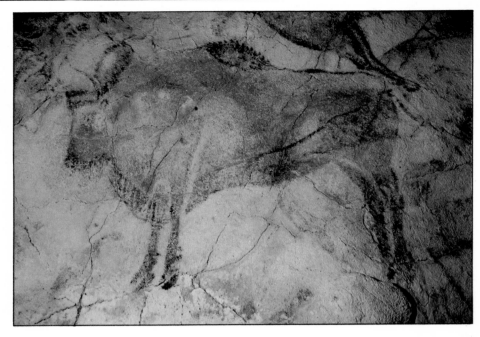

Above: Altamira cave paintings of the Magdalenian people show the advanced stage of art in Spain before 1200 BC.

graved about 27,000 years ago on rock in the Lascaux caves, France. Magic may have inspired art. Possibly artists believed that food-supplying animals would increase if depicted on cave walls.

Australopithecus (southern ape) lived about 4–5 million years ago. He walked upright and probably used bones and stones for immediate purposes before discarding and forgetting them. His remains have been found as far afield as Africa, China, Java and the Middle East.

B **Bones** provided an easily-worked material. The earliest known Chinese

Aborigine with a boomerang

characters are written on skull bones preserved in the National Museum, Taiwan.

Boomerangs, curved, slightly L-shaped sticks made by some ABORIGINES OF AUSTRALIA, proved effective weapons in hunting and war. There were 3 kinds. *Returning boomerangs* were used in contests of skill and for deflecting birds in flight so that they swooped down, to be scooped into a net. *Non-returning boomerangs,* when thrown accurately, killed or maimed human enemies, animals, reptiles, birds and fish. *Ritual*

boomerangs, decorated with secret symbols, were used in dance-mime-song performances and ceremonies. The ancient Egyptians and Hopi 'Indians' of north America also used boomerangs.

C **Civilization** is a word that man, throughout his history, has tried to define. In the broadest sense it can be taken to mean a group of people living together, socially and technically in advance of simple hunters. If, in some great world clock true man arrived 24 hours ago, civilization

began within the last 5 minutes. An 80-year-old person of today has already lived through one-eightieth of the entire span of civilization.

Clans, social groups composed of several families, supposedly descended from a common ancestor. Several clans may form a *tribe*. An intermediate group is called a *phratry*.

Clothes of early man became increasingly sophisticated. Skins were sewn together with needles of bone and thread from sinews of animals and teeth or shells sometimes decorated the

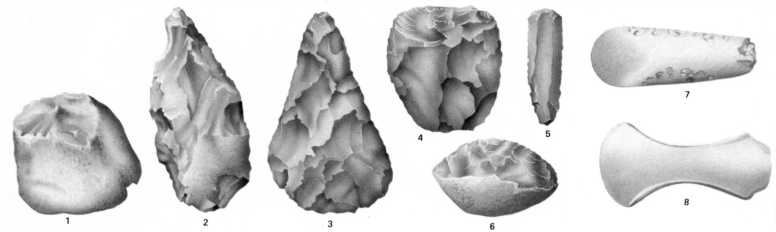

Above: The varied tools of Stone Age man included: **1** pebble chopper (Olduvai Gorge, Tanzania); **2** primitive pointed hand axe with unrefined zig-zag flaking along edge (Fardwick, Kent, U.K.); **3** pointed hand axe (Swanscombe, Kent, U.K.); **4** flaking tool with carefully trimmed edge (Northfleet, Kent, U.K.); **5** knife chopper (Dordogne, France); **6** scraping tool (Dordogne, France); **7** polished axe of the New Stone Age (Mildenhall, Suffolk, U.K.); **8** stone battle axe of the early Bronze Age (Battersea, London, U.K.).

fences supplemented or replaced fire as defences against human or animal marauders.

Perhaps the most important step in man's advance to CIVILIZATION came when he learned to farm. That is, when he sowed seeds to raise crops and domesticated farm ANIMALS. This probably happened in the Middle East about 11,000 years ago, when the taming of the horse is thought to have occurred.

Beginnings of technology

Men's first vehicles were probably the floating logs they clung to, to escape being washed away. Later, they scooped out logs to make early canoes and controlled them with crude paddles. Wooden rollers and levers were used to move heavy stones into position, and large rafts were built to float them downstream. The Sumerians of Mesopotamia used sledges to transport people and materials. With the invention of wheels, animals trained to carry goods could be harnessed to carts.

Man found his earliest materials easily enough. Wood, rushes or earth lay all around him. Dead animals provided furs, skins, BONES, horns and ivory. The need to slice meat and cut and shape materials encouraged men to make the first tools, the earliest being easily-made wooden or bone types. Then men chipped stones into crude knives, axes, hammers and weapons. Flint made the best tools: it could be easily worked into shape and so these were probably the most precious possessions of early people. The first New Stone Age men appeared less than 10,000 years ago in the Middle East. Their improved tools included polished stone axes and flint

sickles which were attached to lower jawbones taken from suitable animals. About 8,500 years ago, people in present-day Turkey and Iran began working copper, but the first bronzesmiths did not appear until civilization had been established in Mesopotamia for 1,000 years.

Social groups

The family pre-dated man: animals had grouped themselves into families long before he emerged. Human families probably comprised three generations, although grandparents would be fortunate to survive beyond their mid-30s. Despite enmities and rivalries, relatives had great incentives to stay together in bands. Large families constituted strong defence units, provided that they did not outstrip available food supplies.

Like animal groups, each tribe looked upon a certain area as its own territory, to be exploited for water, food, shelter and materials. As the human population grew by MIGRATION or natural increase, tribes had to defend their territories against invaders. Inflexible 'laws' governed relationships between members of different tribes and even more rigid rules dictated relationships within each tribe. Certain kinds of behaviour were *taboo,* meaning that they violated a tribe's rules and were therefore banned.

Development of religious ideas

When a tribe numbered several hundred people, the *idea* of it as a social group, rather than as a number of individuals, became difficult to comprehend. To solve this problem, some tribes chose symbols to represent them, for example one group became perhaps the Bear tribe, clearly

---

hems and cuffs of skin garments. Necklaces and bracelets of teeth, shells, mother-of-pearl, and fishbone were carved with intricate patterns.
Counting probably began with the body, which provided a 'ready reckoner'. People noticed that they had 1 nose, 2 hands, 4 limbs, 5 fingers on each hand, and 20 fingers and toes. It was no accident that the system of numbers given to the world by the Indian mathematicians was based on 10, or that the Central Americans used a *vigesimal* system of

numbering, based on 20s.
Cro-Magnon. Some of the earliest remains of modern man, *Homo sapiens sapiens* were found at Cro-Magnon, in the Dordogne area of south-western France. Cro-Magnon man survived until 10,000 years ago.

D **Dancing** and singing gave outlets for people's emotional needs probably before speech developed. So perhaps did the drum, which may have been the first musical instrument.
Didgeridoos and bullroarers, musical instruments

made and played by the ABORIGINES OF AUSTRALIA give an insight into Stone Age music. Didgeridoos are drone pipes made from hollowed wood and painted with secret, sacred designs. By using his lips and tongue, a player created animal or bird-like noises. He maintained a continual sound by breathing in through the nose, while at the same time he breathed out through the mouth. Bullroarers are thin, flat pieces of wood attached to cords. Whirled around the head they make a whirring noise, supposedly the voice

of an ancestral spirit. Strict religious rules governed the use of both these instruments.
Dreamtime, in translation, is the Australian Aborigine's

term for the beginning, when all things were created. They believe that spirits of the unborn come from the Dreamtime and return there at death.

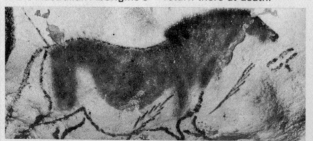

Lascaux Caves painting, Dordogne, France

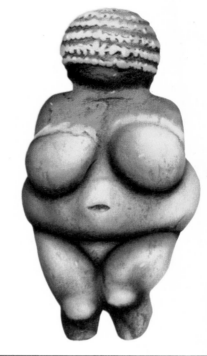

Left: This stone monument is the Dolmen de Kercadoret in Brittany, France. 'Dolmen' is the term used for a type of prehistoric structure that was built as a burial chamber in the Neolithic period. There are many fine examples in Britain and France.

Right: The 'Venus of Willendorf' (Austria) is one of the earliest known works of art. It is a limestone figure, 10 cm high carved perhaps 25,000 years ago to symbolize fertility.

distinguished from the neighbouring Crow people. The images of bear and crow would be the *totems*, or emblems, of the two tribes. Much later, the 'Red Indians' of North America and the Polynesians in New Zealand erected poles with their totems at the top.

Certain natural features within the tribal territory or on the horizon came to be regarded with awe. Natural phenomena such as volcanic eruptions, thunder, lightning, rain, sun, moon and stars, seemed to possess overwhelming power in their own right. Aware of their comparative inferiority, men worshipped them as super-beings, or deities. One deity in particular, the Storm god in the storm-swept Hittite empire, became the chief god. Dead, or even living, leaders became gods in their own right.

Witch doctors emerged, to become the keepers, enforcers and interpreters of tribal behaviour, tradition and magic. Their activities combined simple science with law and superstition. They slew people to gain the gods' favour, but also saved lives by dispensing beneficial herbs or performing simple surgery. Eating a certain animal might be taboo because it possibly either carried disease or, so it was thought, the soul of a dead ancestor.

The universal custom of burying or burning the dead was partly a matter of hygiene, but with burial went the belief in an after-life. People buried their dead with food and a few possessions to comfort them in the next world. Many people believed that the soul of the dead would remain with the tribe.

Man's early method of COUNTING was probably based on the body, when someone noticed

Right: A tomb or *long barrow* built about 4,500 years ago at West Kennett, Wiltshire, U.K., held the bodies of 45 or more people buried at different times. The dead, possibly chieftains, were buried with arrowheads, beads and earthen vessels to comfort them in the after-life. The roof was formed of 50 tonne stone slabs.

E East Africa is believed to have been the home of man's earliest-known ancestors. *1470 man* (named from the catalogue number in the Kenya National Museum) was discovered in 1972. Remains of *Ethiopian man* were unearthed in 1974. Both these early men walked erect and made simple tools.

G Grain of the prehistoric world was mainly wheat, barley, oats and (in the Americas) maize. Other basic crops included lentils, peas and beans.

L Levers were probably first invented by the Magdalenian people of France-Spain some 12,000 to 17,000 years ago. These people also produced the outstanding murals at the Altamira caves, in Spain.
Leisure. Stone Age people probably did not work very hard when the environment became more favourable. They possibly laboured about half the number of hours now worked by people in modern industrial societies. Story-telling would have occupied much of their time after dark. Then

as now, children would have played games, imitating their parents' work: hunting, cooking and so on. Games seem to have been popular and adults probably invented them to occupy the family's spare time and energies. The ancient Central Americans played a ball game before the height of their civilization. Sumer appears always to have had 'table games', suggesting that early forms of them predated its civilization.

M Migration. Primitive men, like animals,

could not live where the climate became too cold, too hot, too wet or too dry. Man's early migrations were almost certainly movements towards more moderate climates and better sources of food supply. One of the greatest migrations of all time began about 30,000 years ago when men walked from Asia into the Americas, over what is now the Bering Strait. About the same time, another people migrated from south-eastern Asia through New Guinea into Australia to form the Aborigines of that country.

Arabia, and Central Asia-Mongolia, are believed to have been the starting points of many migrations.

Aborigine with didgeridoo

how many limbs he had. Some observant people detected a constant pattern in the movements of the sun and moon, while some unknown genius linked the idea of number to the rhythm of heavenly movements and so evolved the concept of time. Someone else linked this to the pattern of weather, a first step to an understanding of the seasons. Much later, these ideas were connected to an annual cycle of agriculture.

Man the freebooter

Trade preceded civilization. Barter in salt and gold between peoples who never spoke or even met, was common in Africa until a few hundred years ago. But not all people traded to satisfy their wants. Some turned to robbery or piracy. Tribal law laid down permissible patterns of behaviour with standardized PUNISHMENT for those judged guilty of breaking it.

An early tax collector was the tribal chief who first thought of exacting payment in kind for travellers to drink at his spring or pass through his territory. Inevitably, not all people accepted the rules and people sometimes revolted against their chief or tribal elders.

Man the organizer

Man had learned much, but knowledge was unevenly spread. Here and there, knowledgeable men lived in favourable environments. About 6,500 years ago, such settlements stood poised for the great leap forward into civilization. Unknown men with new talents began to gather together their strands of knowledge and to persuade their fellows to put learning to practical use. The Sumerians were first off the mark. They established settled agriculture, permanent buildings, and an organized economy, and so they pioneered the first recognizable civilization before 4000 BC.

Above: Stonehenge ('hung-up stones'), built on Salisbury Plain, U.K., about 3,800 years ago, may have been an early observatory, or a temple for sun-worshippers. Its builders constructed Stonehenge with a precision based on accurate knowledge of the sun's movements.

Above right: The men who erected the 28-tonne upright stones first dug an incline to a prepared hole, then they dragged a stone to fall into it. While the hoisters balanced the stone vertically, other workmen packed the giant stone firm.

Right: Once erected, the stones were left to settle before workmen cut the tops to an even height.

Right: Horizontal stones were then erected on wooden scaffolding and a lever system used to lay them across the upright pillars.

N Neanderthal man, whose brain slightly exceeded our own in size, made spearheads and scrapers from pieces of flint. He practised rituals and buried his dead, but there is no evidence that he produced art. The first of several Neanderthal skeletons was found at Neanderthal, near Düsseldorf, Germany, in 1856 and the earliest remains date from between 400,000 and 200,000 years ago.

P Punishment at its simplest was one man's revenge against another. In the case of murder, the dead person's clan or tribe often sought to kill the murderer or another of his group, so starting a blood feud. As social groups grew bigger and more advanced, punishment was used less for revenge, and more to deter others from breaking the 'laws'. It became a mechanism through which rulers enforced obedience to tribal customs. The breaking of a certain taboo brought a specific punishment known in advance of the crime. Law helped to maintain the safe existence of the tribe.

R Races in present times include Caucasoids, Mongoloids and Negroids, to which nearly all the world's peoples belong. However, some groups do not fit easily into these categories or combinations of them. Such groups include the Aborigines of Australia, and the Hottentots, Bushmen and Pygmies of Africa. Many scientists believe that the 3 main races at least, descended from common ancestors. Their marked physical differences are thought to have come about through natural selection and adaptation to different environments.

S Spear-throwers are notched holders from

Cerne Abbas giant, England

the end of which spears can be hurled. They increase the force of a throw by giving additional length to the thrower's arm. Australian Aborigines still use spear-throwers.

W Weapons of Stone Age hunters and fishermen included bows and arrows with heads of wood, bone or flint; slings for stones; barbed prongs; and harpoons. Australian Aborigines used BOOMERANGS and SPEAR-THROWERS (perhaps the world's earliest 'machines').

The Sumerians established the first settled civilization, based on agriculture and trade.
They built the first cities, invented wheeled vehicles, and laid claim to the first usage of
a written language.

The Sumerians

About 6,000 years ago, successive waves of people were migrating into the flat coastal clay and marshlands of what is now Iran and southern Iraq. They called themselves the 'black-headed people', and were probably nomadic shepherds. We know them as the Sumerians and the land in which they settled as the land of Sumer.

The Sumerians established the first recognizable civilization with a workable system of government, and their other achievements include the invention of WHEELED VEHICLES and the use of written language. They developed the scientific practice of agriculture and, on the arts side, evolved a distinctive style of architecture and a complex religion which is reflected in their literature.

The pioneers of civilization

The Sumerians probably conquered and intermixed with an earlier people who had migrated from the Arabian desert and by about 3500 BC, they had established several cities which included ERECH (Uruk), KISH, LAGASH, LARSA, NIPPUR and UR (the best known of the Sumerian cities). These cities were built on land deposited

Above: The map shows Mesopotamia as it may have been in Sumerian times although the present-day Persian (or Arab) Gulf probably extended farther north. Akkad is believed to have been on the Euphrates, near to Kish.

by the life-giving 'twin rivers', the TIGRIS and EUPHRATES, which entered what is now called the Persian Gulf as one waterway, the SHATT-AL-ARAB. The land between the twin rivers was called MESOPOTAMIA, and Sumer lay at its southernmost end. Ur (the ruins of which are now over 160 kilometres inland) may once have stood on the coast.

Although the whole of Sumer shared a common culture, the Sumerian city-states (independent cities with their own kings) seldom united and often fought wars against one another. This sometimes resulted in the formation of small empires that rose and fell as the balance of power shifted from one city-state to the next.

However, Sumer lasted well over 1,000 years before it fell to a Semite warrior people from the north, the AKKADIANS, and even then, Sumerian culture continued to dominate the new empire. Many legends surround the person of the Akkadian leader, Sargon I (c.2637-2582 BC), who was once cup-bearer to the king of Kish, including one story which tells that he was found as a baby floating on the river in a basket made of reeds. (This was supposed to have happened

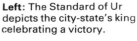

Left: The Standard of Ur depicts the city-state's king celebrating a victory.

Right: The bronze head is probably that of Sargon of Akkad.

Reference

A **Akkadians,** under Sargon I, their humbly-born leader, spread from their capital of Akkad, near KISH on the EUPHRATES, to conquer the whole of MESOPOTAMIA and founded the Akkadian empire which lasted from about 2371-2159 BC. The exact dates are uncertain.
Amorites, a Semitic people from the great desert northwest of Sumer, began to attack and destroy the Akkadian empire from about 2200

BC. About 300 years later, an Amorite prince established himself in Babylon, which became the centre of the Babylonian empire.

B **Burial chamber** of Queen Pu-Abi (or Shubad) was the most interesting of 16 royal graves at UR excavated in the 1920s by Sir Leonard Woolley, a British archaeologist. The sacrifice of human beings at the burial of a royal person such as Pu-Abi was once widespread. Later, effigies were substituted for human attendants.

C **Clay tablets,** inscribed in CUNEIFORM with a sharpened reed, were the usual form of letters and documents in Sumer and were often encased in clay envelopes. Many thousands of these tablets are stored in the British Museum.
Cuneiform (wedge-shaped writing) was developed from pictorial writing by the Sumerians, who may have invented the world's first written language. It was much easier to inscribe cuneiform than pictures on clay, and cuneiform was more precise in meaning.

D **Dumuzi** was the Sumerian name of the god of vegetation known to the Babylonians as Tammuz. Vegetation gods symbolized

A Sumerian god

the course of the seasons: the apparent death of vegetation in winter and its 're-birth' in spring.

E **Elam,** a country at the head of the PERSIAN GULF, lay east of Sumer. Its site is the present-day Iranian province of Khuzestan. The Elamites wrote in cuneiform, which remains undeciphered to this day. Elam's capital, Susa, flourished from 1200 BC, but was destroyed by the Assyrians in 645 BC. Little is known about the early Elamites, except that Sargon's grandson,

approximately 1,000 years before an account was written of Moses having been found in similar circumstances.)

The city of Ur

A fairly typical example of a Sumerian city was Ur, whose inhabitants believed that it belonged to NANNA, the moon god. He lived, they thought, in the north-western corner of the city which stood higher than the rest and was surrounded by a wall. In this sacred area—a city within a city—the citizens of Ur built many temples for Nanna and also a ZIGGURAT (a square-sided tower), at the top of which Nanna was supposed to live with his wife Nin-Gal. People came to the sacred area not only to visit the temples but also to pay their rents and taxes to the god and to receive justice from him. Although they dealt with officials, the citizens regarded them as mere agents of Nanna, and the priest-king who ruled over the city-state was called his steward.

The ziggurat stood solid like a mountain on the flat plain so that far outside the safety of the city, farmers and herdsmen could see Nanna's abode and take comfort that he was watching over them and protecting them.

The oval-shaped inner city of Ur was a maze of narrow streets, alleys and bazaars. The outer city, five times as big, covered only five square kilometres yet housed about 350,000 people, most of whom were reasonably prosperous and traded in locally-produced or imported goods.

Houses were of clay bricks, either sun-dried or kiln-baked, built round a central courtyard to give privacy. In the courtyard there was a drain to catch the rain-water from the sloping roofs. Houses with an upper floor had a wooden balcony connecting the rooms from the outside of the house, but this was only for the rich as Sumer was built on clay and trees were scarce, though stone was even more rare and costly.

Death and the after-life

Each house had a shrine dedicated to the family's own special deity, who guarded its interests. Wealthy people had statues made of themselves, which they stood in the temples to act as their representatives before the gods whom they would pray to and appease while their owners were about their daily business.

Sumer had many deities and myths. DUMUZI,

Right: Sumer's clay-brick cities were not built to last long. Lacking building stone, the Sumerians had to be continually rebuilding. The ruined mounds, or *tells,* can still be found in the Mesopotamian desert. Bricks were either sun-dried or kiln-baked. Other civilizations, including Egypt, may have borrowed architectural ideas from Sumer, the world's first known civilization.

Below: The 'ram caught in a thicket', made of gold, shell and lapis lazuli, is typical of Sumerian art. The 'thicket' may represent the 'tree of life' from Sumerian religion.

Right: A plan of the city of Ur.
1. Ziggurat
2. Wall of Nebuchadnezzar
3. Courtyard of the Temple of Nanna
4. Site of the early Temple of Nin-gal
5. Houses from the time of Abraham
6. Site of Palace of Ur-Nammu
7. The Cyrus Gate
8. The Early Cemetery

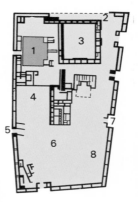

King Gilgamesh of Erech

god of vegetation, was believed to die in winter and to be reborn each spring. ENLIL, whose shrine stood in the city-state of Nippur, supposedly separated heaven from earth. He had many other jobs and the Sumerians believed that he created lesser gods to help him in his tasks. ENKI, a practical god who brought order out of chaos, organized agriculture and engineering.

Although the Sumerians believed in an afterlife, their idea of the next world was not attractive. In it, people sat in darkness eating dust and clay, clothed in feathers like birds. Rich and powerful people took great care to enter the next world in the proper way. When Queen Pu-Abi died over 4,500 years ago, her body was dressed in finery and jewellery and taken to a special BURIAL CHAMBER accompanied by two personal attendants, musicians, courtiers, soldiers and servants. Oxen and donkeys walked

down the ramp pulling brightly-decorated carts and were guided by their drivers and grooms into position in the tomb, where the whole company took up their proper positions and then drank a drug that made them unconscious. When all was still, workmen killed the animals and walled up the chamber, entombing the living with the dead. Queen Pu-Abi had entered the next world in the style demanded by her rank.

Language, literature and crafts
The Sumerians developed the earliest-known written language. Beginning with PICTOGRAPHS (picture writing), they gradually changed to CUNEIFORM (wedge-shaped writing) that could be quickly inscribed on damp clay tablets with a sharp-ended reed, clay and reeds being the two materials that Sumer abounded in. Thousands of these tablets still survive. The Sumerians also

Above: A silver vase depicting the goddess Ningal, wife of Nanna.

Above: Objects recovered from the royal cemetery at Ur include the decorated dagger and the gold beaker shown. The beaker is from the grave of Queen Pu-Abi of Ur, whose burial chamber is the best-preserved of all the royal graves.

Left: The drawing shows the ziggurat at Ur as it may have looked. In hill-less Ur, it loomed like a mountain. Nanna, god and supposed owner of the city-state, was believed to live at its summit. From that vantage point he watched over and protected from evil, those who worked outside the city's walls.

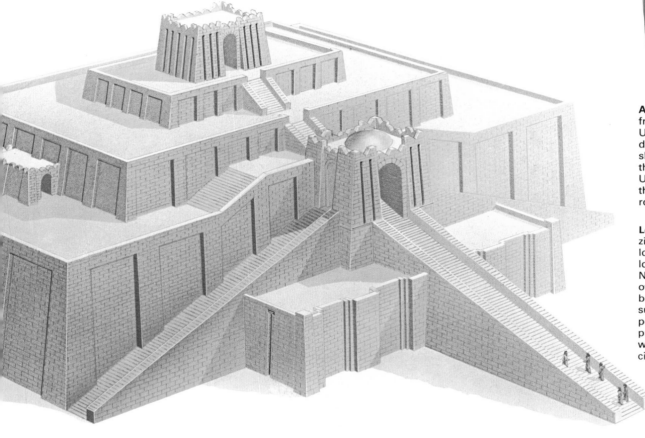

The name was in use until about AD 1920.
Myths are traditional stories often told to explain ideas that are too complex to understand easily. They are found in religion and literature and often involve gods, semi-divine humans and heroes such as ENKI, Utnapishtim and Gilgamesh. Most peoples have devised myths to explain the existence of the sun, moon and stars, the creation of the world, the coming of men and animals, and the development of agriculture and engineering.

N Nanna (or Sin), the moon god, was also the god of Ur, to whom the city-state was believed to

Clay tablet from Lagash

belong. Nanna was also the chief star god. Sumerians believed he rode across the night sky in a quffah (circular boat) accompanied by stars and planets.
Naram-Sin, grandson of Sargon, expanded the Akkadian empire in the 2200s BC, and reigned for 37 years. After his death, the empire disintegrated, mainly under attacks from the Gutians.
Nippur, which lies 145 km south-east of Babylon, was the leading Sumerian holy city. For this reason it never became a city-state, but the

king of the current ruling city-state of Sumeria traditionally claimed it as his own and made a pilgrimage there to receive the blessing of its god, ENLIL.

P Persian Gulf, known to some countries as the Arab Gulf, is a deep inlet of the Arabian Sea, separating Iran from Arabia. Near its northernmost point it receives the waters of the SHATT-AL-ARAB, which deposit silt, from its swampy delta. Some scholars believe that the silt deposits have moved the Mesopotamian coast

much further south than in Sumerian times, and that the site of Ur, now over 160 km inland, may have originally been on the coast.
Pictographs (picture writing) were used to convey messages and meanings before alphabetic languages evolved. Simple pictographs represented concepts such as man, woman, sun, moon and water. In most civilizations, pictographs were replaced by symbols to indicate letters of an alphabet. Nearly all languages, other than Chinese and Japanese, have developed in this way.

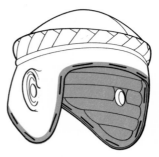

Above and right: The ceremonial helmet *(right)* belonged to King Mes-kalam-du of Ur, and was buried with him. An inner quilting *(above)* was laced into the helmet through the holes in its rim.

Left: Naram-Sin of Akkad is shown on this stele in triumph over an Iraqi king.

Below: The grimmer side of the Standard of Ur shows the city-state at war. It 'reads' from the bottom row upwards. Chariots advance, trampling defeated enemies underfoot. Light infantry armed with axes and spears butcher their naked opponents. Copper-helmeted heavy infantry in cloaks advance ominously. Finally, the king (taller than other figures), confronts the bound prisoners brought before him for judgement. A dwarf holds the reins of the asses which pull the king's war chariot. The pictures show that Sumer was a well-armed military power.

made use of cylinder SEALS for official or business documents which, when rolled over a tablet, left an impression of the pictograph or cuneiform on the seal.

SUMERIAN LITERATURE included the EPIC OF GILGAMESH (legendary king of Erech), in which Gilgamesh mourns the death of his friend Enkidu, who had been created by the gods. Determined to find out how to become immortal, Gilgamesh travels to the Ocean of Death, beyond which he meets Utnapishtim, a semi-divine immortal, who tells him how the gods created a great flood to destroy mankind because they were too noisy. But one god, Ea, warned Utnapishtim of the coming disaster and he escaped by building a boat.

Although the gods were angry at this, Ea persuaded them to grant Utnapishtim immortality. Utnapishtim tells Gilgamesh that the gift of immortality lies in a certain plant. Gilgamesh finds this plant only to be robbed of it by a snake. In despair, he realizes that the gods will not grant immortality to men and that all must age and die.

SUMERIAN ART had a livelier style than that of some other early civilizations, and some splendid examples of it remain. Amongst these is a well-preserved box known as the STANDARD OF UR, which shows the city-state in peace on one side, and at war on the grimmer reverse side.

Other relics of Sumerian art include some magnificent musical instruments such as lyres and harps and some exquisite jewellery made of gold, pearls, cornelian and lapis lazuli, a brilliant blue stone.

Left: The jewels on this model head were once worn by a Sumerian lady. The leaves, flowers and earrings are of beaten gold. The necklace is of cornelian, pearls, and lapis lazuli.

Below: This ivory gaming board has 14 counters, but no one knows how the game was played. The Sumerians seem to have valued their leisure, for several games and musical instruments have been found.

Agriculture and science

The Sumerians may have been the first people to understand the principles of scientific agriculture—the relationship between seeds, soil, water, and the annual cycle of the weather. Barley, their chief crop, was used as a form of money, and they also cultivated flax, lentils, peas, wheat and vetch (a kind of bean), and possibly olives, grapes and other fruits.

To improve agriculture, Sumerian engineers constructed dams and canals, which were also used for water transport. Silt from the river fertilized the land which yielded two crops a year. The Sumerians kept sheep and goats and some pigs—animals considered to be unclean and eaten only by the poor.

The Sumerians took a great interest in mathematics, possibly out of the necessity to survey land. They based their number systems on units of 60 and passed on to present times the 60-minute hour and the 360° circle.

Akkad takes over Sumer

About 1,000 years after civilization began in Sumer, Sargon of Akkad conquered the warring city-states and set up the Akkadian empire which lasted for about 200 years (2371-c.2159 BC). Sargon's first triumph was to make himself king of the city of Akkad, after which he added Kish to his domains. Many battles later, he defeated Erech, broke its walls, and took its king in chains to Nippur. His campaigns took him far and wide, from the backward land of Assyria to the north, to Lebanon (known as the 'land of the cedars' as it supplied so much timber) and to the Mediter-

ranean Sea. He also claimed the conquest of ELAM, a country to the east.

Sargon's main aim in fighting these bloody and exhausting wars seems to have been the sheer glory of conquest, though he was also motivated by the need to gain raw materials such as wood, stone and metals, and to expand his foreign trade on favourable terms. He was history's first great empire builder and his reign lasted for about 56 years, after which he was followed by his grandson, NARAM-SIN (reigned c. 2260-2223 BC), who extended the empire. On the death of Naram-Sin the empire began to decline and break up. Erech rebelled and seized much of the old land of Sumer; the AMORITES attacked from the north-west; but the most powerful attack came from the fair-skinned, barbarian Gutians, who pushed in from the Zagros mountains. The Sumerians called them the 'Mountain dragons' and by about 2160 BC they ruled much of Mesopotamia.

Opposition to the Gutians came from the city-state of Lagash, whose priest-king, Gudea, (reigned c. 2143-2124 BC), halted the Gutian advance. Gudea kept his city-state at peace, preferring prosperity to conquest, but after his death, Sumer came under the leadership of the king of Erech, who finally drove out the Gutians. The Sumerian-Akkadian territories became increasingly unstable politically, and by 2000 BC the Amorites were taking over the city-states.

Despite political and military upheaval, Sumerian civilization did not die. It was absorbed by Babylonia, and later by Assyria, and its influence was felt as far afield as Egypt.

Above: A golden bull's head found buried at Ur once adorned a lyre. Experts rebuilt the instrument as it was.

Above; Sumerian seals, when rolled across documents, left a pictographic or cuneiform impression.

Above: Sumerians wrote on clay with a sharp reed. The pictographs gradually developed into cuneiform.

The Curse of Agade (Akkad), which may have been sung to the music of the lyre. The greatest work of Sumerian literature is the EPIC OF GILGAMESH.

T Tigris, a river rising in eastern Turkey, flows over1,800 km south-east into Mesopotamia to unite with the Euphrates and form the Shatt-al-Arab.

U Ur, the best known of the Sumerian cities and traditionally the original home of Abraham, 'father' of the Jews, was excavated by

Gudea, priest-king of Lagash

Sir Leonard Woolley in the 1920s. Its many important finds included the royal burial chambers.
Uruk, see ERECH.

W Wheeled vehicles were probably first invented in Sumer, where they took over from sleds and were in use by about 3250 BC. They were made from 3 pieces of wood and were bound together with wooden battens and leather.

Z Ziggurats, square brick pyramids with steps leading upwards, dominated

Sumerian toy on wheels

most Sumerian cities. In the hill-less plain of Sumer, the complex structure of the ziggurat looked like an artificial

mountain, and was believed to be the dwelling place of the city-state god.

The majesty of the pyramids at Giza is just one of the many wonders left behind by the Egyptian dynasties. The chance discovery of Tutankhamun's priceless treasures has re-awakened our interest in this fascinating era.

The Egyptians

The Egyptians depended upon the Nile River for life even more than the Sumerians relied upon the twin rivers, the Tigris and the Euphrates. The Nile Valley *was* Egypt – a thin ribbon of fertile land hemmed in by sandy desert. The Egyptians became master builders, competent agriculturalists and mathematicians and they established the world's first nation-state. Much of their achievements derived from their obsessive concern with life after death.

The isolated nation-state

HAMITIC PEOPLE began farming along the valley and delta of the Nile about 6,000 years ago. By about 3100 BC, when they had established several small estates, King Menes united the south and the north in one long narrow kingdom extending about 900 kilometres along the Nile. MEMPHIS became the capital soon after 3000 BC.

Egypt regarded its king, or PHARAOH, as a GOD-KING, not as the representative of a god like the Sumerian priest-kings, but as a god in his own right. To govern effectively, the pharaohs divided Egypt into *nomes* (districts), each under a governor.

Above: The map shows that the towns of Egypt lay near the Nile. Egypt lies at the cross-roads of 3 continents.

Surrounded by deserts and seas, Egypt was sheltered from raids and invasions for 1,400 years, and its isolated civilization remained almost unchanged for twice that long. Historians have divided Egypt's history between 3100 and 332 BC into 31 royal periods, or DYNASTIES.

The pyramids

The best known feature of ancient Egypt is its pyramids, the earliest of which was built for King Zoser (Djoser) of the 3rd dynasty by IMHOTEP, the first architect named in history. This was a step pyramid located at SAQQARA, near the Nile, south of present-day Cairo, and represented the world's first stone monument. Around the Saqqara pyramid, Imhotep built several courts and temples. Although stone was used for royal and official buildings, such as the pyramids, ordinary Egyptians lived in simple mud-brick houses.

The great pyramids built during the 4th dynasty were located at Giza, now a suburb of Cairo. The two largest were built in the 2500s BC for King KHUFU (Cheops) and his son King KHAEFRE (Chephren). The mysterious sphinx car-

Below: Stone masons found plenty of suitable material along the Nile Valley.

Below: Levelling the site according to the surveyor's instructions was the first job in building monuments.

Reference

and scorpions were believed to belong to the god SETH.

Anubis was the jackal-headed god. His role was to weigh human souls in the balance against the feather of Truth. He was also believed to preside over funeral rites, the dead, and open the roads to the next world.

Asia Minor was the name used in ancient times to describe the area now roughly covered by Turkey. The Hittite civilization developed there about 1900 BC.

A **Alexander the Great,** king of Macedonia, mastered Greece and took Egypt in 332 BC. After his death, one of his generals, Ptolemy, became pharaoh, and Ptolemaic Egypt lasted from 304 to 31 BC.

Animals played a leading role in the mythology of Egypt. Several important deities took the form of animals or had animal heads, and antelopes, asses, boars, crocodiles, hippopotamuses

Illustration on papyrus of animals

C **Carter,** Howard (1874–1939), a British Egyptologist employed by Lord Carnarvon, discovered the tomb of King TUTANKHAMUN in November 1922. It took Carter 10 years to clear the tomb which was packed full with precious objects.

D **Double crown** of Egypt was worn by kings and pharaohs from the time of Menes (reigned

c.3100 BC). Pharaohs had a choice of 4 crowns. The conical-shaped white crown represented Upper Egypt, the serpent crown represented Lower Egypt. These 2 were combined into 1 and worn as the double crown, denoting the unity of the country. The fourth was the blue war crown.

Dynasties of Egypt, with approximate dates, were as follows (all BC):

1st	3100–2890
2nd	2890–2686
3rd	2686–2613
4th	2613–2494
5th	2494–2345

Left: The sphinx has a lion's body but a human face, said to be that of Khaefre, 4th king of the 4th Dynasty. The monument is about 4,500 years old and was carved out of a rocky outcrop.

Right: The pyramids at Giza were built as royal tombs. Three of them are much larger than the others. The 'Great Pyramid' of Khufu is probably the largest building ever constructed. Next to it is Khaefre's pyramid. Next to that (smaller) is Menkare's pyramid behind the 3 small pyramids of queens in the foreground.

ved for Khaefre is believed to have his likeness. These monuments are among man's greatest but most useless achievements. Built as tombs for the pharaohs, the massive pyramids wasted the energies of the nation. To construct Khufu's tomb-pyramid, 100,000 slaves laboured for 20 years, shaping and moving into position about 2,300,000 blocks of stone weighing about two-and-a-half tonnes each. The base of the pyramid is large enough to enclose six football fields. It is a true square to within 15 millimetres accuracy – a tribute to Egyptian skill in mathematics and surveying.

The Egyptian hierarchy

Below the pharaoh, enforcing his will, were the nobles, priests and officials. Chief among the officials, the vizier enforced the law and imposed social and economic order. A vast army of conscientious scribes, or clerks, assisted the officials in controlling agriculture, industry and trade.

Below: Inside the Great Pyramid, burial chambers (1) and (2) were never completed. The real funeral chamber (3), past the grand gallery (4), was ventilated by shafts (5) and (6). After burial, the corridor (7) was sealed from within by lowering stone 'plugs' *(right)*. The workmen then escaped through the shaft (8) and the corridor (9).

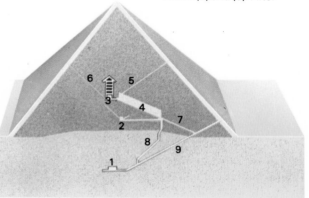

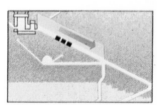

Below: Earth ramps may have been built around the stone pyramids, forming (as in Sumerian ziggurats) sloping paths along which the stones could be dragged to the top.

Below: Moving the massive blocks of stone made heavy demands on human muscle power. Rollers probably eased the burden but pyramid builders did not have pulleys.

E **Egyptian art.** The 2-dimensional art of Egypt was often very detailed, and many pictures require close study, especially in the case of religious pictures. These often tell a complex story, and sometimes have HIERO-GLYPHICS incorporated into them to explain what is happening. Sculpture, though stiff, is often expressive and always distinctive. Early

Tomb of Nakht

Egyptian buildings were made of solid stone blocks accurately positioned, as in the pyramids. Later buildings had massive lintels supported on tall columns, like those at KARNAK and Luxor. Tomb architecture was intricate, and was more akin to engineering than to art. A great variety of delightful artistic craftwork can be seen in the contents of TUTANKHAMUN'S tomb.
Egyptian literature varies from poems and narratives written for pleasure to the *Book of the Dead*, which was written on papyrus and buried with the dead. It was regarded as a magic charm that would protect them against danger on their journey to the next world. Many

Book of the Dead

Above: Farming, the chief occupation of the Egyptians, was almost entirely carried out along the fertile banks and the delta of the Nile. Many crops were cultivated, including grains, fruits and vegetables. Wine and beer were produced. Scribes forecast the quality of the harvest by measuring the level of the Nile's water. The volume of water largely determined the harvest.

Right: A fellah (Egyptian farmer of present times) ploughs his land with an ox team, using methods unchanged for thousands of years. About 6 out of every 10 Egyptian workers still till the soil or raise animals. Agriculture produces 30 per cent of the gross national product. A pharaoh looking at a present-day field might think (but for the change in dress) he was in his own time.

Below: Irrigation canals flow between plots of cultivated land along the Nile Valley. In Egypt the source of all life is still the Nile. Rainfall is almost non-existent. Many times in their history the Egyptians have dammed the Nile. This has expanded the volume of water for irrigation, so increasing the crop yield.

Taxation and trade

In the almost rainless country, agriculture depended upon the volume of the Nile's waters. NILOMETERS were installed to measure the rise of the river, and so enable the size of the coming harvest to be predicted. The scribes then estimated the likely tax yield, and from this sum, they alloted funds to various government departments to finance new development projects. Scribes also set up check points on the Nile, which was by far the most important trade route, and searched the boats like modern customs men, exacting taxes for the pharaoh.

Apart from stone, Egypt relied heavily upon imported raw materials. Up the Nile from the Mediterranean came timber from Lebanon; semi-precious stones such as malachite and turquoise came from Sinai; copper from Cyprus; and tin, iron, gold and wine from ASIA MINOR and the LEVANT. Down the Nile from Nubia came amethyst and gold; and from east Africa, animals and animal products.

Agriculture

Most Egyptians toiled on the land. They seldom went hungry and their food was varied, but even those who were not actually slaves were often

Right: The shaduf, a simple but effective device for irrigation, has been used in Egypt for 3,500 years. Water is drawn from the Nile or one of its canals into a bucket attached to a weighted pole. The weight lifts the full bucket, which can then be easily emptied into a tank built at a higher level. From the tank, water is channelled through small 'canals' to irrigate land some distance from the river. The canals slope downwards, using the power of gravity.

Egyptian tales, most of them incorporating myths and legends, have been published in English.

El Fayum, west of the Nile, is a low-lying oasis with a lake fed by a canal from the Nile. It was considered to have an ideal climate for crop-growing. Pharaohs of the 12th dynasty irrigated the area and developed it into the garden of Egypt.

Engineers in Egypt first developed technology from the need to control the water of the Nile. They constructed dykes, dams and canals to curb harmful flooding and to

provide irrigation, and their skills were also needed in the construction of the country's complex buildings.

Ethiopians, a darker, Hamite people, joined with

Howard Carter

the Nubians to conquer Egypt about 750 BC. Their leader, Piankhi, (c.751–716 BC), took Thebes, which had become semi-independent, before pushing on to Memphis where he founded the 25th dynasty. This is sometimes called the Kushite (Cushite) dynasty after the region of Kush in Nubia-Ethiopia.

F Forced labour was drawn from several classes apart from slaves. Prisoners of war, especially from Nubia and southwestern Asia, and even

freemen were conscripted for special projects like flood-control or the construction of pyramids and canals. Slaves could be bought and sold, but were allowed to own property and rent land, though serfs were bound to a particular estate and usually sold with it. Generally, Egyptians were not conscripted for the army, which relied mainly on mercenaries, who were mostly Nubians, Libyans and Sherden (an Aegean people).

G God-king. A pharaoh was believed to be the

falcon god Horus, son of OSIRIS, master of the sky, whose rebirth he symbolized. To the Egyptians, the sky was a huge falcon with

Pharaoh (right) of Egypt

Right: Surveyors measure a field with their ropes. Accurate land surveying was regarded as highly important by Egypt's rulers. Apart from planning development projects, officials wanted to know the exact size of plots of land in order to tax them justly. Some plots held by smallholders were about 5 hectares. Others plots were 25% or 50% of that area.

Right: A plough team cuts a furrow. The plough came into use in Egypt about 4,500 years ago (when the pyramids were built). At first it was little more than a 2-handled hoe with a shaft added. It took another 1,000 years before the plough had a metal share. Handles were then strengthened by the addition of more cross pieces. Speedier ploughing released men for new trades.

pressed into FORCED LABOUR for the pharaoh. Canals, pyramids, palaces, tombs and temples had to be built and maintained. An unknown scribe recorded the grievances of ancient Egypt's peasants, deploring especially the taxes they had to pay.

Barley, wheat, fruit and vegetables were staple crops. Dates, figs, leeks, onions, garlic, cucumbers, radishes, beans and lettuces were grown and eaten even by the poor. Wine was produced from the plentiful vineyards and beer made from barley. As Egypt increased in prosperity, many peasants' sons became artisans, and contemporary friezes show the work of bakers, brewers, butchers, carpenters, metal workers as well as many others.

The quest for agricultural efficiency turned Egypt's priests and officials into competent scientists and ENGINEERS. They studied mathematics to become accurate surveyors, correctly interpreted the seasons and the annual growth cycle, and calculated that the year had 365 days. They built dykes and dams and IRRIGATION canals, especially at EL FAYUM.

Egypt's architects built on a grand scale. About 1,000 years after the pyramid builders, they constructed mighty temples and tombs at

Above: Ancient Egyptian fishermen on the Nile land a good catch. Fish (which cost nothing) was eaten gladly by poor people, even though it was sacred.

Left: Present-day Egyptians search for fish offshore. Using little equipment they seek free food as the price of their labour. Their ancestors did the same in Pharaonic times.

the sun and the moon for eyes. They believed that Horus's judgement was infallible and that he was 'served by the dwellers of heaven', according to an ancient poem. They also believed that justice was 'what Pharaoh loves', and injustice 'what Pharaoh hates'. To encourage the people to worship them, the pharaohs of the New Kingdom (18th–20th dynasties) had huge statues erected to themselves.

H Hamitic people lived in the Hamitic language belt which extends across northern Africa from Morocco to the Indian Ocean. Their languages include Berber, Kushitic, Somali and Hausa, which are all closely related to Semitic languages, such as Arabic.

Hathor, Egyptian sky goddess, is often represented as having a cow's head, or a woman's head with cow's ears or horns. She was the protectress of women and the dead, and goddess of love, joy and fun. On New Year's Day priestesses dragged Hathor's image from the temple into the first light of dawn to symbolize that the day of celebration and merriment could begin.

Hieroglyphics were a form of ancient writing which was

Rosetta Stone hieroglyphics

common in Egypt before 3000 BC, and also used by other races including the Indus Valley people, the Hittites, Aegeans, Mayas and Aztecs. Hieroglyphics developed from pictographs, where things were represented by their images. When papyrus was introduced as a writing material in conjunction with an ink made of gum or soot, hieroglyphics became more cursive, or flowing. It was possible to write faster, and to describe more complex things, with signs representing different syllables. *De-*

motic hieroglyphics (from democratic – available to all) were the most advanced form developed by the Egyptians. Simpler and quicker for ordinary people to understand, they continued them even after they had designed an alphabet of 24 letters.

Horus, see GOD-KING.

Hyksos, people from southwestern Asia, are said to have migrated from Syria, into Egypt. There they seized power in about 1674 BC and ruled from Memphis, until they were expelled in 1567 BC. They were also called the 'Shepherd Kings', and

THEBES, a royal city and burial ground which lay nearly 700 kilometres south of the pyramids.

Ancient Thebes covered some 16 square kilometres. On the east bank of the Nile stood the city of the living, including the great temple of KARNAK, which began to be built during the 12th dynasty (1900s BC) and was still being added to 1,600 years later. The smaller Luxor temple was built about 1400 BC.

City of the dead

Across the Nile on the west bank at Thebes (modern Luxor), lay the 'CITY OF THE DEAD'. Most burials and cemeteries in ancient Egypt were made on the west bank of the Nile in the desert so as not to waste valuable agricultural land and because the Egyptian equivalent of heaven was thought to be in the west with the setting sun. One of the titles of Osiris, the god of the dead, was 'Lord of the Westerners'. At Thebes nobles had brightly decorated tomb-chapels cut into the hillside; the burial chamber with the mummy was deep below them. In the 18th dynasty the pharaohs began to be buried in a remote valley in the Theban Hills now known as the VALLEY OF THE KINGS. The first pharaoh buried there was Thothmes I in c.1512 BC, and most of the pharaohs of the next two dynasties were also buried there. Each tomb is now numbered and the last one found, number 62, is that of TUTANKHAMUN.

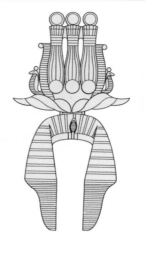

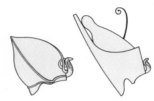

Left: Pharaohs had a choice of the ceremonial crown *(top)*; the white crown of Upper Egypt *(centre right)*; the red crown of Lower Egypt *(centre left)*; the double crown *(bottom right)*; or the blue war crown *(bottom left)*.

Above: A solid gold mask covered the head of King Tutankhamun's mummy. The false beard, snake and vulture are royal symbols.

The hall of the Egyptian gods

Isis, the wife of Osiris	Ra, the sun god	Anubis, the guide of human souls	Hathor, the sky goddess	Seth, the god of all animals	Thoth, messenger of the gods

founded the 15th and 16th dynasties.

Imhotep, counsellor of King Zoser, was a priest, a doctor and an architect, and the people also regarded him as a magician. Together, Zoser and Imhotep constructed the world's oldest-known stone building, the step-pyramid at SAQQARA. It dates from c.2670 BC and was surrounded by temples and courts.

Irrigation in Egypt was largely carried out using the 'basin system'. The cultivated ground was divided

Temple of Hatshepsut

into huge areas made into basins by the construction of solid enclosing walls, and when the Nile was in flood, water was diverted into the basins by canals. From each basin (which might cover up to 17,000 hectares) water was channelled into outlying areas. In gardens and orchards, water was hand lifted until the invention of the *shaduf* – a bucket swung on a counter-weighted pail.

Isis, wife and sister of OSIRIS, was the mother of Horus. She collected the pieces of her murdered husband and reassembled him.

K **Karnak,** on the east bank of the Nile, the northernmost point of THEBES, was the site of 3

temples, much of which still stands, including the temple complex of Amun-Re (the sun god), one of the largest in the world. Its construction began during the 12th dynasty. The arch was not used in Egypt, and the roof was

Colossi of Memnon

Most of the royal tombs were robbed of their rich contents centuries ago. Several of them stood open in classical times and Greek and Roman tourist have left their names and comments scribbled on some of the walls.

In the tombs of the nobles the walls are decorated with colourful and lively scenes of everyday life, work in the fields and such-like. The bright paintings in the tombs of the kings are only concerned with scenes of the king in the company of the gods, and extracts from various religious books such as the *Book of that which is in the Underworld.*

It is a curious fact that modern scholars have learnt much of what we know of the daily life of the ancient Egyptians from their way of death; from the detailed painted and carved scenes on the walls and from the many objects placed in the tombs for their owners use in the afterworld. They sincerely believed that they were going to a far better world.

Religion and mythology

Religion played an important part in Egyptian society. Some of its many deities were believed to control birth and death, while others were responsible for various aspects of daily life: surveying, language, numbers, harvesting and so on. Egypt had two supreme gods, RA (Re) and OSIRIS. In Egyptian mythology, the good god Osiris was killed by his twin brother SETH, who

cut his body into pieces. ISIS, wife of Osiris, put his body back together again, so the god was resurrected. Osiris, Isis and their son HORUS, a falcon god, formed a trinity at the top of the pantheon. Their chief helpers included ANUBIS, jackal-headed god of the dead; THOTH; the ibis-headed scribe; and HATHOR, the cow goddess. The role of Anubis was to weigh the heart of each dead person against a feather (symbolizing Truth) on the scales. Monsters devoured those

Left: Four giant statues of Ramses II were carved from the rock at Abu Simbel. 3 of the 4 (one lost its head) stared across the Nile for 3,200 years. Then they were cut from the rock and lifted by mechanical means in AD 1964. To save them from flooding caused by the construction of the Aswan High Dam, they were resited nearby.

Above: The throne of King Tutankhamun, made of wood and decorated with gold, shows the king sitting at leisure attended by his wife. They are blessed by the sun's rays.

Nepthys, protective goddess

Horus, the sky god

Osiris, the god of the dead

Ptah, the god of Memphis

Sobek, the god of crocodiles

Amon, Lord of the Thrones of the Two Lands

---

supported by massive lintels on top of giant columns. The great *hypostyle* (pillar-supported) hall was a floor 118 x 52 metres with 134 columns arranged in 16 rows.
Khaefre (reigned c.2540 BC), 4th king of the 4th dynasty, built the 2nd largest pyramid at Giza, and probably also constructed the sphinx.
Khufu (or Cheops, reigned c.2560 BC), 2nd King of the 4th dynasty, erected the largest of the Giza pyramids nearly 5,000 years ago.
Kingdom. Ancient Egyptian history is divided into the

following kingdoms:

Period	Dynasties
Archaic	1st-2nd
Old Kingdom	3rd-6th
1st Intermediate	7th-10th
Middle Kingdom	11th-12th
2nd Intermediate	13th-17th
New Kingdom	18th-20th
Late	21st onwards

L **Levant** is the name used to describe the area from the coast of the eastern Mediterranean, inland to the Nile, Tigris and Euphrates. It has no precise boundaries.
Libyans. Berber tribes from Libya began to attack Egypt during the 19th dynasty, and

settled in the delta area west of MEMPHIS. When they were expelled in the 20th dynasty, many returned to become mercenaries in the Egyptian army.

Ram-headed sphinxes

Lower Egypt covers the small delta area between Cairo-Giza and the Mediterranean.

M **Macedon** (or Macedonia), the northern part of Greece, dominated Greece by 338 BC, and in 332 BC ALEXANDER THE GREAT set out to conquer Egypt, where one of his generals founded the Ptolemaic dynasty in 304 BC.
Mathematics, geometry and trigonometry were developed by Egyptian priests and officials for use in surveying, irrigation and building. Because the Egyptians

were only interested in the applied sciences, it was left to the Mesopotamians to develop them further.

Obelisk, Luxor

Above: Many animals were considered sacred in ancient Egypt. The falcon was one of the highest divinities and represented the idea of 'god' in pictograms.

Below: The Egyptians believed that a man needed his body in the after-life so they preserved the dead by the complex procedure of embalming and mummification.

Right: Archaeologists discovered the tomb of King Tutankhamun, dating from 1352 BC, remarkably undamaged by time and robbers.

found to have unjust hearts, whereas good-hearted people were allowed to enter into the after-life.

The traditional religion was disturbed by King Amenophis IV (reigned c.1375-1358 BC), of the 18th dynasty, who changed his name to Akhenaton to symbolize the beginning of a new religion based on the worship of one god only: Aton, the sun. But priests forced his next-but-one successor, Tutankhamun, to restore the old religion within 20 years.

Mummies

A strange custom practised by the Egyptians was mummification, the preservation of dead bodies. The brain and internal organs, excluding the heart, were first removed from the body. Then the body, excluding the head, was steeped in a solution of salt or natron for several weeks. The body was then washed, covered with preservatives and swathed in bandages. The whole process took 70 days.

The art of mummification reached its height during the 21st and 22nd dynasties, and its purpose was to try to preserve as much as possible of a person's identity after death. The idea of a person disappearing into nothing horrified the Egyptians, who even mummified some animals.

Egyptian writing

The waterplant papyrus grew freely in Egypt, providing material for sandals, mats and sailcloth. Above all, it provided a useful writing material similar to paper. A sharpened rush made a pen, and gum and soot were used as ink. Having papyrus instead of clay, the Egyptians had no need to use cuneiform. Instead they developed pictographs into clearer HIERO-GLYPHICS.

Early hieroglyphics were pictographs, which later became more abstracted so that they could be written more quickly. Hieroglyphics were carved on the temples and monuments of Egypt, where they can still be read. By about AD 500 they had been forgotten and were regarded only as magical signs through which evil could be communicated. But in the 1820s Jean Champollion, a Frenchman, deciphered them using the ROSETTA STONE.

Arts of Egypt

Ancient EGYPTIAN LITERATURE includes mythological or historical romances, poems, essays on morality, school texts, and political propaganda. A popular work, *The Story of the Shipwrecked Sailor*, tells how a sailor became a castaway on an island in the Red Sea, and was given shelter by a strange serpent. *The Tale of the Two Brothers* seems to be connected with the myth of OSIRIS and SETH. In the *Tale of Sinuhe*, a fugitive from Egypt settles in Palestine among the desert nomads. In old age, he is pardoned and allowed to go home.

EGYPTIAN ART forms were varied. However, one rather rigid but fascinating style predominated. Pyramid and temple architecture still stands solid and visual arts can be seen in the many statues, especially those of Pharaoh RAMESES II, and papyrus paintings, which are usually religious in theme. The Egyptians were also fine jewellers, and a wonderful collection of artistic craftwork was found in 1923 when the British Egyptologist Howard CARTER opened the tomb of the teenage pharaoh, Tutankhamun of the 18th dynasty.

History

The kingdom ruled by Menes about 3100 BC comprised UPPER EGYPT and LOWER EGYPT, and to symbolize the unity of the two countries the pharaohs wore a DOUBLE CROWN. The most famous of all the pharaohs is perhaps Rameses II of the 19th dynasty. The Egyptian dynasties ruled for about 1,400 years, after which the Semitic HYKSOS people trickled into Egypt from Syria about 1674 BC and eventually seized the royal power.

The Hyksos lasted 100 years and then the Egyptians ruled until the LIBYANS, who were employed as soldiers by Egypt, seized power to form the 22nd dynasty. This began a long series of disastrous invasions, and the Nubians and ETHIOPIANS ruled Egypt as the 25th dynasty. They were followed by the Assyrians who invaded Egypt and set up the 26th dynasty. The Assyrians were defeated by the Persians, who founded the 27th dynasty. The 31st and final Persian dynasty fell to ALEXANDER THE GREAT of MACEDON in 332 BC. Nevertheless, this was not the end of the Egyptian civilization, which lived on under its new conqueror.

Below: This necklace represents the scarab-god rolling the ball of the sun into the other world, just as the scarab-beetle pushes a ball of dung. He symbolized the renewal of life and the idea of eternity.

Left: This gilded wood statue of Tutankhamun as a harpooner is one of many statues symbolizing the king's after-life.

portance when a Theban family established the 11th dynasty. Later it became the royal residence of pharaohs of the 18th, 19th and 20th dynasties. When Thebes was the capital of the 25th dynasty, it was sacked by the Assyrians and fell into decline. It is the site of the Luxor and Karnak temples and the royal tombs.

Thoth, divine vizier of OSIRIS and later of Horus, was a god with many functions. He was inventor of all sciences and arts, messenger of the gods, moon god, and keeper of the divine records. Usually shown with the head of an ibis, Thoth is also sometimes represented as a dog-headed ape.

Tutankhamun was one of the last kings of the 18th dynasty. A boy king, he died at the age of 18. His tomb was discovered in 1922 in the Valley of the Kings near Luxor by Howard CARTER.

U **Upper Egypt** is the 1,500 km strip of the Nile Valley between Cairo and Egypt's border with Sudan.

V **Valley of the Kings** was the area of ancient Thebes lying on the west bank of the Nile. Fearful that tomb robbers would take away their comforts in the after-life, the pharaohs had their tombs constructed underground with a maze of shafts and passages designed specially to conceal the tomb entrance and mislead the robbers. The tomb of Queen Hatshepsut (reigned 1503-1482 BC), for example, is over 200 metres from the entrance and nearly 100 metres below ground. Certain nobles were also entombed in the Valley of the Kings.

Step pyramid, Saqqara

The Indus Valley was a rich, fertile land that bore a wealth of agricultural produce. The civilization which grew up there thrived for 1,000 years before mysteriously disappearing without trace.

The Indus Valley People

Above: This statuette of a bearded man — possibly a priest-king — found at Mohenjo daro, is one of the few remaining sculptures from the Indus Valley civilization.

One of the three great 'river civilizations' developed along the valley of the INDUS RIVER in what is now Pakistan. It began about 4,500 years ago and covered a vast area of over a million square kilometres. Some 60 to a 100 separate settlements grew up, centred around HARAPPA to the north and MOHENJO DARO to the south. These two cities each had a perimeter of about five kilometres.

In those days the Indus Valley was much more fertile than it is today. Some scholars believe this is due to a change of climate and that heavy rain once fell in areas now arid. Others think that it is the soil that has deteriorated because the inhabitants felled too many trees and overgrazed sheep and goats. Like the Sumerians and Egyptians, the Indus Valley settlers depended upon yearly silt-bearing floods to irrigate the land. These came in March when snow and glaciers melted in the mountains to the north.

Harappa and Mohenjo daro, of which more

Above: The map shows that the Indus Valley people lived in the region made fertile by the 5 rivers of the Punjab feeding the Indus. Place names refer to present times except for Harappa and Mohenjo daro.

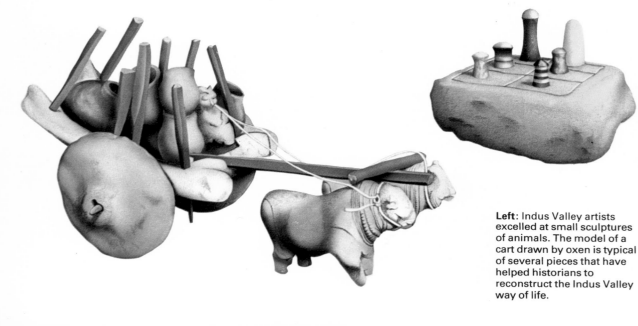

Left: Indus Valley artists excelled at small sculptures of animals. The model of a cart drawn by oxen is typical of several pieces that have helped historians to reconstruct the Indus Valley way of life.

Left: Gaming 'boards' made of solid stone entertained those who had time for leisure in the Indus Valley. Players probably moved the pieces (*shown*) across the 'board' to play a game similar to draughts. This gaming board is much less refined than those found in Sumer.

Reference

A **Amulets** were popular in most ancient civilizations. They were small objects worn as charms to ward off evil.
Aryan people probably began migrating from central Asia about 2000 BC. One branch pushed westwards into Europe, while another moved into the Indus Valley, whose civilization had probably been weakened by natural causes before they destroyed it by war about 1500 BC. The story of how the lighter-skinned Aryans conquered the darker-skinned native population is told in Indian literature. Most Indians, Iranians and Europeans are largely descended from these Aryan (or Aryan-speaking) people.

Beads from Mohenjo daro

C **Cotton**, grown widely in the Indus Valley, was spun and woven into cloth for clothes. The methods used changed little until the present century. It is possible that the Indus Valley people were the first to produce cotton cloth. The Egyptians of the same period wore linen.

G **Granaries** were of great importance in the ancient civilizations, where wheat and barley often served as currency. No coins have been found in the Indus Valley, where it is likely that definite weights of wheat grain were used instead of money. The granaries were therefore the 'treasuries', grain playing the part of gold and silver in later civilizations.

H **Harappa**, one of the two main cities of the Indus Valley civilization, stands on the old bed of the Ravi River (south of the present course), about 600 km north-east of Mohenjo daro. The city had a strongly fortified citadel with watchtowers, and was laid out on a grid system. Harappa was thickly populated and workmen lived in lines of barrack-like houses. A dominating building in the city was the granary, covering nearly 3,000 square metres. The ruins of Harappa were largely demolished in 1865, when John and William Brunton, 2 British engineers, used bricks from the ancient city as ballast for the railway they were building from Lahore to Karachi.

Below: The artist's reconstruction of the now-ruined 'great bath' of Mohenjo daro suggests similarities with the huge tanks found in later Hindu temples. The 12 x 7 metres bath was waterproofed with bitumen and fitted with a good drainage system. Bathers entered it at each end, down wide brick stairs with wooden treads.

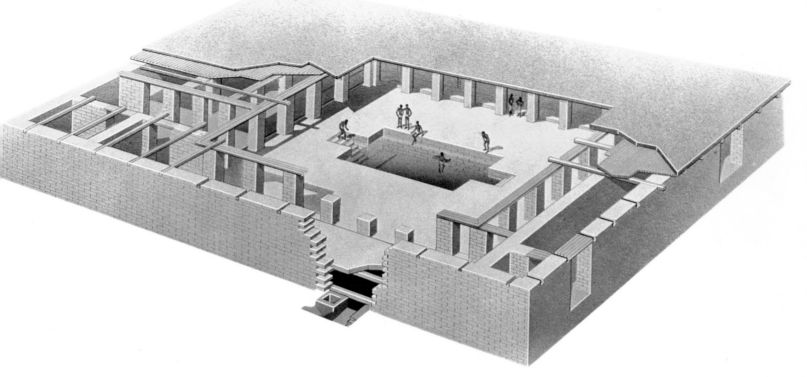

has survived, were both highly-planned cities with wide roads and houses of fired brick. The Indus Valley people excelled at drainage and sanitation. Their houses had private bathrooms drained by earthenware pipes running to main drains under the streets and into huge sump pits. A great public bath has been uncovered at Mohenjo daro and there were many wells.

Mohenjo daro and other Indus Valley cities were planned on a grid system and laid out with precision. No previous civilization had taken town planning so seriously. Houses mostly had at least two floors and were of plain brick without decoration. Roads were wide — often nine metres across and sidewalks were unpaved and dusty. TEMPLE ARCHITECTURE was unimpressive compared with that of Egypt and Sumer.

Government and trade

Little is known about the form that government took in the Indus Valley, although the standardized pattern of town planning suggests that Indus Valley settlements had a strong central government like Egypt. Harappa and Mohenjo daro were quite possibly both capital cities.

WEIGHTS and measures were also standardized, according to archaeologists, and this gives us a fuller picture of the economic life of the people. On a local scale, farmers probably transported their surplus crops to towns in oxcarts to exchange them for such wares as pottery, copper or bronze axes, fish hooks, razors and weapons.

The Indus Valley was fertile but possessed few raw materials, so the people imported certain goods. Imports were paid for by exporting surplus food. Single-masted sailing boats with oars brought copper from what is now the Persian Gulf. Camel and donkey caravans would have brought bitumen and steatite from

Above: The elaborate drainage system of Mohenjo daro provides evidence of town planning by a central authority imposing high standards of hygiene. Drains had manholes at intervals, allowing workmen to clear them of rubbish.

I **Indus River** rises at an altitude of over 5,000 metres in the Kailas range in Tibet, north of the Himalayas. Its length is about 2,700 km. It flows north-west for about 1,000 km, passes through the Himalayas, and then through Punjab and Sind in Pakistan. After flowing through the Thar Desert it is fed by the waters of the '5 rivers of the Punjab': the Jhelum, Chenab, Ravi, Beas and Sutlej.
Indus Valley settlers. Skeletons found in a cemetery at Harappa suggest that 2 basic races of Indus

Valley men existed. Most were tall (about 1·75 metres) and Caucasoid in appearance. Others were smaller with finer features and 'Mediterranean' looks. One Mongoloid skeleton was also found in the cemetery.

M **Mohenjo daro** lay about 600 km southeast of Harappa, but unlike the latter, Mohenjo daro escaped vandalism. The site has been only partly excavated. The city had a fortified citadel like the one at Harappa, which it resembled in several ways.

R **Rajasthan,** now a state of India covering roughly the old state of Rajputana, borders present-day Pakistan. It lay about 150 km from the main Indus Valley cities.
Ritual bathing, which now dominates the life of the

The ruins of Harappa

Indian city of Benares (Varanasi), was practised just as fervently in the Indus Valley settlements. Apart from its hygienic value, bathing is a purification ceremony. It is as essential to Hinduism as it was to the religion of the Indus Valley people.

S **Script** in the Indus Valley was pictographic and not alphabetical. About 400 signs have been found, and some have only recently been deciphered. The script ran in lines that probably read from right to left, below that left to right, then right to

Sign	Object	Meaning
⋎		possession
⋏		'star', Mars
∧		black
⋀	2 previous signs combined	black star
⋔		lord
⊟		woman, female

Far left: Indus Valley pictograms had misleading meanings. For example, the pictogram *roof* in the Dravidian language of the Indus Valley had the name *mey*, but it also served to mean *mai*, which, translated, meant *black*.

Above: These scales were used to weigh goods in the Indus Valley and similar ones can be found today. Weights were based on the bright red seed of the gunja plant, conventionally fixed at 0·118 grammes. Officials strictly controlled weights.

Baluchistan, silver from Afghanistan, and lead from RAJASTHAN. Indus Valley people almost certainly traded with the Sumerians, and the two cultures may have been related because pictures have been discovered which show that they wore quite similar clothing and hairstyles.

Language, arts and religion

The Indus Valley people used a pictographic SCRIPT which remains undeciphered to this day. It can still be seen on SEALS, pottery and amulets. The art of the Indus Valley was not outstanding, though some STATUETTES do have a certain graceful style. Jewellery was produced from gold, silver, lapis lazuli and precious stones such as amethysts.

Religion

Religion links the Indus Valley civilization to later periods in Indian history. The god SIVA was worshipped, bulls were sacred, and RITUAL BATHING was almost an obsession. On some seals Siva is shown as a three-headed god, lord of all the beasts.

Agriculture

Indus Valley farmers grew wheat, barley, rice, mustard, sesame, dates, melons and cotton, and they raised cattle, water buffaloes, sheep and pigs. Elephants, camels and horses may have been used as beasts of burden, while cats and dogs were kept both as pets and as working animals. Each city had a huge granary which stocked grain, just as later treasuries hoarded gold.

Decline and fall

The Indus Valley civilization lasted about 1,000 years before it declined and vanished. No one knows for certain why it fell; perhaps the land became infertile or the population outstripped its food supply. It is believed that the coastal areas rose in relation to the sea, so causing flooding inland. A combination of these factors would have weakened the Indus Valley people, leaving them an easy prey for invaders. ARYAN PEOPLE from the north-west probably destroyed the civilization by war about 1500 BC. Only its religion survived.

Above: The lively copper statuette of a dancing girl found at Mohenjo daro displays the vitality characteristic of later Indian sculpture. It is 10 cm high.

left, and so on. There is no indication that the pictographs were developed into cursive or CUNEIFORM writing, *(see page 11)* as in Mesopotamia.

Seals were common in the Indus Valley and many have survived. The motif is often an animal and occasionally a god in a square design. About 4 to 8 pictographs usually appeared above the symbol.

Siva, most important of the Hindu gods, was worshipped in the pre-Hindu Indus Valley settlements. The god is shown on some surviving seals in the form of Pasupati, lord of beasts. Several animals attend him. He has 3 faces, possibly symbolizing that he combines the roles of creator, preserver and destroyer. He sits on a low stool and wears a large horned headdress, which probably signifies his close association with the sacred bull. (Nandi, Siva's bull, is among the most worshipped of idols in present-day India.)

Statuettes found in the Indus Valley sites are among the best pieces of the civilization's art. Most impressive of all is the bronze figurine of a dancing girl.

T Temple architecture so far excavated in the

Granaries at Harappa

Indus Valley is small in scale. Religious buildings seem to have been small shrines rather than massive structures like those that dominated Sumerian and Egyptian cities. The religious buildings discovered by archaeologists differ little from ordinary houses.

W War does not seem to have been a dominant feature of the Indus Valley civilization and few weapons have been found. This fact alone would explain why foreign invaders might have made an easy conquest.

Weights were standardized throughout all the Indus settlements and few fraudulent ones have been found, suggesting that strict control of trading was enforced. Weighing followed a binary system, the ratio being: 1, 2, 4, 8, 16, 32, 64. Weights were usually made of polished stone such as alabaster, limestone and jasper.

The Aegeans founded the fabulous Greek civilization which gave the world its treasury of mythology, art and legends, such as the story of the Minotaur, the topless towers of Ilium and the lost city of Atlantis.

The Aegean Peoples

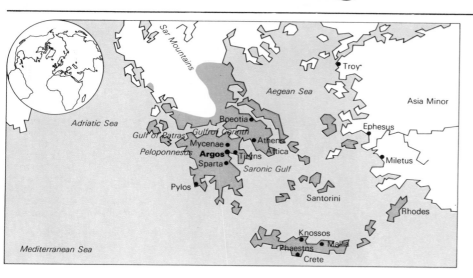

Above: The map shows that the Aegean civilization centred round the Peloponnesus and adjacent parts of Greece, and spread into the Aegean.

The AEGEAN CIVILIZATION of the eastern Mediterranean has two centres: the island of Crete and MYCENAE in the south-east area of the Greek mainland. Scholars differ in their opinions as to whether we should think of the Aegean as one civilization or two. No one knows where the early Cretans came from, but they may have been related to the HITTITES who lived in what is now Turkey. The Cretans were among the earliest peoples to make BRONZE tools and weapons (about 3000 BC). They were also called Minoans, after MINOS, their legendary king.

Beginnings
While the Cretans were establishing a civilization around their capital city of KNOSSOS, several tribes were moving southwards across Greece and by 2000 BC, a Greek mainland civilization was in being at Mycenae.

The Aegean lands had dry, hot summers and wet, mild winters. Mountains dominated both centres and only 20 per cent of the land was fit for cultivation. This limited the population and encouraged the Aegeans to look to the sea. The Cretans came to dominate the sea routes of the eastern Mediterranean and the Mycenaeans gained a reputation for piracy.

The Cretans founded the first civilization in Europe – the ancestor of the present Western civilization. Our knowledge of the Aegean civilization, though scanty, owes much to the work of two archaeologists: Heinrich SCHLIEMANN, who began to excavate Mycenae in 1876; and Sir Arthur EVANS, who began digging at Knossos in 1900.

Language
The solution to several mysteries about Crete may lie in its language. Archaeologists found two scripts in Crete, both inscribed on tablets of clay and written in syllabic scripts. Scholars called the oldest script LINEAR A and the other LINEAR B. Linear A has never been deciphered, but Linear B, deciphered in 1951, is the language of Mycenae. The Mycenaeans may have destroyed the Cretans in war and replaced the Linear A script with their own Linear B. But some scholars believe that Linear B was used in Crete long before Knossos was destroyed in 1400 BC.

Religion
Although the religions of Crete and Mycenae differ, their mythologies have several points of contact and both are part of the great mythology of the Greek world. A gold signet ring from Crete shows a woman praying by a pillar as a god descends from the sky. Cretan deities appeared in human form and dress, and people burnt sacrifices to them from hilltop shrines. Generally little is known about the religion of either Crete or Mycenae, though it is certain that the deities of Mycenae included the chief god, ZEUS, and his sea-god brother, POSEIDON. It is likely that the Mycenaean religion was an early form of the religion practised later by the Greeks.

Reference

A **Achaeans** were among the earliest fair-skinned people to enter Greece about 2000 BC. Sometimes the Greeks referred to themselves generally as Achaeans, though for the Hittites, the Achaeans were the people of a small kingdom on or near Rhodes.
Acrobats, or dancers of both sexes are shown somersaulting over huge bulls in pictures from Crete. The first bull acrobats were of the royal family; later, slaves performed the ceremony. Possibly it was a ritual designed to appease the 'earth bull' believed to be responsible for earthquakes.
Aegean civilization centred around the Aegean Sea — especially Crete and the Greek mainland settlements of Mycenae. It began in Crete about 3000 BC. When Cretan cities were destroyed about 1400 BC, Mycenae became the strongest Aegean power. Dorian Greeks conquered Mycenae and the Aegean civilization ended about 1000 BC.

Arcadians, one of the first fair-skinned people to invade Greece (about 2000 BC), settled in the north-central Peloponnesus. Hun-

Minoan gold jewellery

dreds of years later they led the resistance to warlike Sparta.
Argos, 10 km south of Mycenae, was a Mycenaean citadel set on 2 hills. It had no warrior-nobles of its own.
Artistic craftsmen of Crete were famed throughout the eastern Mediterranean for their gold jewellery, marble vases, and beads of *faience* (a form of glazed earthenware).
Athens was already a place of some importance when Mycenae was at the height of its power and it already had a citadel on top of its acropolis. In mythology, THESEUS left from Athens to slay the Minotaur.
Atlantis is mentioned in the works of the Greek philosopher Plato as the 'lost continent'. In mythology, when the gods shared out the Earth, POSEIDON received a paradise called Atlantis, but its people became corrupt and threatened to dominate the whole world, so ZEUS planned their downfall. One night the sea swallowed up Atlantis in an earthquake. Possibly the real Atlantis was the island of Santorini (Thera), north of Crete.

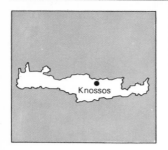
Left: The location map shows that Knossos lay close to the centre of the northern coast of the island of Crete.

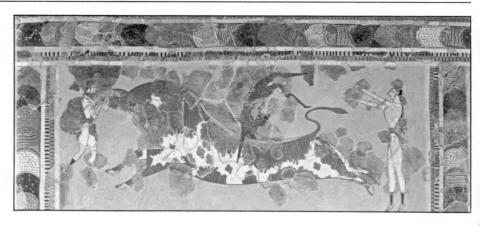

The Cretans built four great palaces: the largest at KNOSSOS, the others at MALLIA, PHAESTOS and Kato Zakro. The palace at Knossos (covering 20,000 square metres) was a maze of halls, stairways, courts and chambers, each designed for a special purpose. There were bathrooms and water closets, and a system of drainage through terra-cotta pipes. Life at court is described in pictures that have survived from Knossos. Some of the most interesting frescoes from the Knossos palace show ACROBATS somersaulting over the horns of giant bulls in some dangerous sport ritual. Royal families seem to have enjoyed a leisurely life and their palaces were unfortified. Court dicing tables inlaid with gold and ivory were among the impressive works of Crete's ARTISTIC CRAFTSMEN.

Above: A fresco from Knossos shows highly-skilled acrobats somersaulting dangerosly over a bull. Bull cults were common in early civilizations from Crete to Assyria.

Mythology of Crete
The mythology of the Cretans suggests that they were in close contact with the Greek mainland. Minos, legendary king of Crete, was believed to be the son of Zeus and the goddess EUROPA. He became king of Crete when, in answer to his prayer, Poseidon sent him a sacrificial bull from the sea. (Bulls figure prominently in Cretan mythology and were probably sacred in its religion.) The wife of Minos gave birth to a Minotaur — a bull-headed man who was imprisoned in a maze called the LABYRINTH. To punish the Greeks of ATHENS for murdering one of his sons, Minos decreed that every ninth year (some say every year) they must provide seven youths and seven girls to feed the Minotaur. The monster was eventually killed by one of the intended victims, an Athenian hero named THESEUS.

Evidently the bull was a powerful symbol to the Cretans. Some scholars suggest that it signified the terrifying power of destructive earthquakes that perpetually rocked the island.

Attica, in south-eastern Greece, lay north-east of Mycenae and the Peloponnesus. Athens was founded near its southern shore.

B Boeotians, one of the early fair-skinned invading tribes in Greece, set up the kingdom of Boeotia north-west of Attica. Long after the end of the Aegean civilization, Boeotia became the persistent enemy of Athens.

Bronze, a tough alloy composed of copper and a small quantity of tin, was first worked by the metalsmiths of Mesopotamia about 3000 BC. Knowledge of the new metal spread quickly to Crete, where metalsmiths put it to good use. But Crete was not rich in metals and soon had to import copper from Cyprus and tin from Spain.

D Dorians began to invade Greece in force about 1150 BC, though they had migrated into Greece before this. They conquered the Peloponnesus, Crete and Rhodes and ended the Mycenaean civilization. They may have introduced iron tools and weapons into Greece.

E Europa in mythology was the daughter of a king of Phoenicia. ZEUS fell in love with her, appeared in the form of a bull, and carried her out to sea and off to Crete. She married Zeus and gave birth to MINOS.

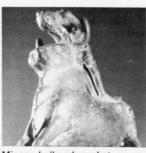
Minoan bull and acrobat

Evans, Sir Arthur (1851–1941) was a British archaeologist who began excavations in Crete in 1893 and at Knossos in 1900. His most noteworthy achievement was the almost total reconstruction of the palace of Knossos — present knowledge of the Cretan civilization comes largely from this work, but later scholars have criticized his methods.

Sir Arthur Evans

H Hittites, an Indo-Aryan people of Asia Minor, dominated the Middle East for over 700 years between

Below: Knossos, the capital of the legendary King Minos, was one of the greatest cities of the ancient world, with a population in the region of 100,000. As Knossos increased in prosperity, building started on its magnificent and complex palace, in 1900 BC. The discovery of the ruins of the palace by Sir Arthur Evans was one of the most note-worthy events in our century. He found that the palace covered some 20,000 sq. metres and consisted of buildings with 2, 3, 4, and 5 storeys. Thick columns, some painted black, some red and some white supported the various layers and majestic staircases led to the higher levels and roofs. The sacred emblem of Crete, the horns of the bull, topped the roofs. Made of stone and painted gold, they shone brightly in the hot sun. The palace abounded in royal apartments, storage rooms and shrines built around a central paved courtyard.

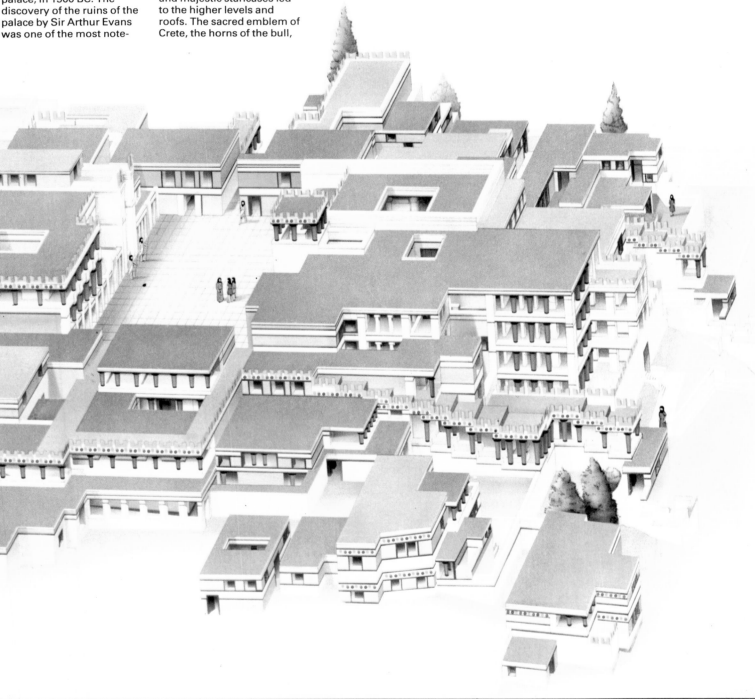

2000 and 1200 BC. *(See page 38.)*

Homer was said to be a blind Greek poet who lived about 800 BC. He is tradition-ally regarded as the author of the *Iliad* and the *Odyssey*, but some scholars believe that he collected and ar-ranged his 2 epics from earlier material. Others doubt whether there ever was an author named Homer, but if he did exist, he was the first known Euro-pean writer.

Iliad, one of Homer's 2 great epics, consists of 24 sections which relate a 7-week episode in the Trojan war. The central hero is Achilles, a Greek warrior. When Achilles's comman-der, King Agamemnon, takes from him a beautiful girl captive, Achilles sulks and refuses to fight, and the Greeks suffer defeats. Even-tually, Achilles re-enters the battle and kills Hector, the Trojan leader. Hector was the son of King Priam and was also the brother of Paris, who supposedly caused the war by kidnapping or elop-ing with Helen, wife of King Menelaus of Sparta.

Illyrians, one of the later invaders of Greece, settled in the western Balkans by about 1000 BC. At one time their power extended from the Danube River to the Adriatic Sea and the Sar Mountains. Later, they oc-cupied the 'heel' of Italy for a while. Some merged with the Macedonians.

Ionians, an invading tribe,

Achilles slaying a Trojan

settled in central Greece. They later fled from the Dorians into Attica, where some became the ancestors of the Athenians. Others sailed to the coast of Asia Minor and founded 12 towns, including Ephesus and Miletus.

K **Knossos** was probably founded by the Cretans about 3000 BC. After it de-veloped into a city it was twice destroyed by earth-quakes and twice rebuilt. The third (capital) city of Knossos, with its harbour town, may have housed

History of Crete

For about 550 years (1950 to 1400 BC) the Cretans enjoyed a golden age. They needed few soldiers on the island because the sea gave protection from the invasions suffered by most other civilizations. Although earthquakes twice destroyed Knossos, the industrious Cretans rebuilt it, each time better than before. Knossos became the largest European city of its time, with an estimated population of 100,000.

Crete's rulers were probably priest-kings, and there may at one time have been a city-state system rather than a unified central government. The country was self-sufficient in food, providing a diet of fish, meat and various vegetables. Both wine and beer were drunk.

Control of the sea routes was the basis of Cretan power and influence. Several pictures and lead and clay models have survived, showing that Cretan ships were masted and of low freeboard. Cretan seamen brought tin from Spain to supply the island's skilled metalworkers, and gold, pearls and ivory from northern Africa to be fashioned into jewellery. Cretan craftwork was much prized abroad, being superior to that of most neighbouring peoples. Craft products were exported especially to mainland Greece and Egypt, together with olive oil. Cretan sailors established colonies on other islands, including one at RHODES dating from about 1600 BC.

Suddenly, about 1400 BC, the palaces of Crete crashed into ruins. No one knows whether to attribute the destruction to an earthquake or a human enemy like the Myceneans. However, about that time the Cretan-owned island of Santorini (also called Thera, some 125

Above: The *labrys*, or double axe was a sacred symbol of the Minoans. It gave its name to the mythical Labyrinth – the complex maze in which the legendary Minotaur lived.

kilometres north of Crete) exploded in one of the biggest volcanic eruptions known to history. Possibly the resulting tidal wave and ash fallout destroyed Cretan civilization. Some people believe that the sudden disappearance of much of Santorini below the waves may be the real story of the 'lost continent of ATLANTIS'.

If Crete survived the catastrophe of about 1400 BC at all, it was as a much weakened state, fast declining. In art and craft at least, the decline had set in before 1400 BC. The centre of power in the eastern Mediterranean passed to Mycenae and the Cretan civilization perished.

Mycenae

The Mycenaeans were generally a taller and tougher people than the Cretans. Living on the

Right: Snake goddesses were common features of the Cretan and Egyptian civilizations. The priestess of the Cretan snake goddess or earth mother was widely worshipped in caves and hilltop shrines.

Left: These clay tablets show the Cretan script known as Linear A. Sir Arthur Evans was the first to recognize these hieroglyphics, but they remain as yet, undeciphered.

100,000 people. Its splendid palace, covering 20,000 square metres, flourished some 3,500 years ago. Knossos and the other Cretan cities were destroyed mysteriously about 1400 BC.

L **Labyrinth** was the complex maze in which the Minotaur lived. When THESEUS entered the Labyrinth to kill the Minotaur he payed out a ball of thread given him by Ariadne, daughter of MINOS. Thus he was able to find his way out after the killing. The legend of the Labyrinth may have

been inspired by the maze-like construction of Knossos Palace. The Labyrinth was named after the Cretan double axe (*labrys*).

West Magazines – Knossos

Linear A is the older of 2 scripts discovered in Crete. It was written in syllabic form (each sign representing a syllable) and has not been deciphered.

Linear B is the later of 2 scripts found by archaeologists in Crete. Michael Ventris, a British architect, deciphered it in 1951, and found it to be an early form of Greek.

M **Mallia,** one of the chief cities of Crete, had a palace smaller but similar to that of KNOSSOS. Several fine private houses belonging to

aristocrats have been excavated there.

Minos, legendary king of Crete, appears prominently in Greek mythology. Several myths surround him, his wife Pasiphae, and his children. Minos is said to have been the first to bring Crete under one ruler. Possibly he was a real person whose awesome power encouraged others to weave stories around his name.

Mycenae has 2 meanings: the city, based on the palace citadel; and the much larger territory controlled by or in alliance with the My-

cenaeans. The independently ruled kingdom of PYLOS, for example, is referred to as part of Mycenae.

O **Odyssey,** one of Homer's 2 great epics, tells of the adventures of Odysseus (Ulysses) during his return from the Trojan war and the problems he faced on his homecoming.

P **Peloponnesus** is the peninsula of Greece south of the gulfs of Patras, Corinth and Saronic. It is linked to Attica by the Isthmus of Corinth. It was the

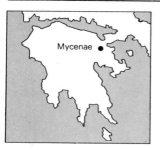

Left: The location map shows that Mycenae lay in the Peloponnesus, near to the land bridge with Attica.

Left: In 1876 the archaeoiogist Heinrich Schliemann found the gold mask of a Mycenaean of rank who lived 3,500 years ago. He mistakenly believed it to be the mask of Agamemnon. Cretans probably took the idea of mask-making from Egypt.

mainland they had to jostle with other tribes for the limited territory available and with their advanced bronze weapons they easily conquered the stone-age farmers of south-eastern Greece. By 1900 BC they had established fortress towns at MYCENAE, PYLOS, ARGOS, TIRYNS and other sites from which they commanded the land and the nearby sea.

Little is known about the political and social structure of the Mycenaean world, though it may have been organized around city-states. Popula-

Below: The grave circle at Mycenae enclosed 6 royal tombs hewn vertically out of the rock. Archaeologists found 19 skeletons in them.

isk from Phaestos

eartland of the Aegean ivilization on the mainland. haestos, one of the lead-g Cretan cities, had a alace smaller but similar to

the one at KNOSSOS. Some 3,000 seal imprints on clay found at Phaestos have contributed to our knowledge of ancient Crete.

Pylos was one of the chief Mycenaean towns. LINEAR B tablets found at Pylos reveal that a person's status there was measured by amounts of grain. For example, the king was said to be worth 30 units of grain, his minister 10, and so on.

Poseidon, god of the sea and brother of the sky-god ZEUS, was called Neptune by the Romans. He was worshipped by mariners be-

cause he was thought to have the power to create storms.

R **Rhodes,** an island between Crete and Asia Minor, was colonized by the Cretans about 1600 BC. It was colonized again by Dorians from Argos some time before 1000 BC.

S **Schliemann,** Heinrich (1822–90) was a wealthy German businessman who devoted his life to archaeology. Fascinated by Homer's *Iliad,* he began to excavate TROY in 1871 and started on

Mycenae in 1876.
Spices and flavourings enlivened the dull, cereal-based diet of the Mycenaeans. They included co-

Schliemann's wife, Sophie

riander, sesame, celery, mint and cress.

T **Talanton** or *talent* was the unit of weight in Crete. It had 2 values: 25.86 kg and 37.80 kg. Volume was measured by the *cup.*

Theseus, an Athenian, was one of the intended victims of the Minotaur. When he landed in Crete, Ariadne (daughter of King MINOS) fell in love with him and helped him to kill the Minotaur. Theseus later abandoned Ariadne on Naxos to the god Dionysos, but became king

Above: The blade of this magnificent Mycenaean dagger inlaid with gold and silver shows nobles attacking 3 powerful lions.

tions were tiny. The kingdom of Pylos had perhaps 200 settlements containing 50,000 people. It was divided into 16 units, each controlled by a governor. Below the Mycenaean court, with its top-ranking nobles and officials, was a class of second-rank, land-holding nobles. Below them were the 'working class' and a class of slaves, most of whom were women, probably seized after their menfolk had been killed in some battle or act of piracy.

Trade, agriculture and crafts
The Mycenaeans (like the Cretans) traded mainly by barter, but barley, and possibly ceremonial axe-heads, passed as a kind of money. The Mycenaeans had a simple number system which, strangely, lacked a symbol for zero. Mycenaean weights were based on the TALANTON, which had two values: 25.86 and 37.80 kilogrammes.

The main crops were barley and, as agricultural methods improved, wheat. SPICES added flavour to the dull diet. Olives, figs and vines were cultivated and bees kept for honey. Small horses, oxen, cattle, pigs, goats and sheep were raised. These provided transport and haulage, food and milk, wool, hides and other products. Specialized tradesmen included coastguards, masons, furniture makers, and an obscure group called 'blue glass paste makers'.

The lion gate palace
Just about the time that Knossos fell (about 1400 BC), the kings of Mycenae rebuilt their hilltop palace-citadel. Impressive entrance gates were built into the walls. One, still standing has a massive lintel topped by a triangular block carved with two lions against a column. Outside the walls, huge beehive-shaped tombs were constructed.

Within the palace the rulers lived comfortably, but less luxuriously than the earlier rulers of Knossos. The Mycenaean court jewellery was superb in quality and may have been Cretan in origin or modelled on Cretan jewellery.

Mythology, legend and history
Mythology, legend and history are intertwined in our knowledge of Mycenae. Much of it comes from two great epics, the ILIAD and the ODYSSEY by the Greek poet HOMER, who wrote 600 years after Mycenaean power had reached its peak.

Historians know that several fair-skinned tribes began to conquer the darker-skinned people of the Greek mainland about 4,000 years ago. The invading tribes included ARCADIANS, ACHAEANS, IONIANS, BOEOTIANS, DORIANS, ILLYRIANS, and THRACIANS. Having subdued much of southern Greece between 1400 and 1200 BC, the Mycenaeans turned to conquests overseas. They attacked TROY in Asia Minor which, according to tradition, fell in 1184 after a ten-year siege. In Homer's epics, the TROJAN WAR was fought because of the love between a Trojan prince and the queen of Sparta. In fact, the Trojan war was probably fought over trade rivalries.

New waves of Dorian Greeks attacked the Mycenaean towns about 1000 BC. The victorious Dorians intermixed with the Mycenaeans, who disappeared from history. The Peloponnesus fell, and only ATTICA kept its freedom. Mainland Europe's first civilization was at an end.

Above: The long Trojan War was finally brought to a close when Ulysses cunningly built a wooden horse, packed it with soldiers, and left it as a gift outside the gates of Troy. He knew the Trojans would take it inside. The Greek soldiers inside the horse came out at night and let their comrades into the city.

of Athens. Many other stories are told about Theseus, including one that he was Poseidon's son.
Thracians, one of the tribes that invaded Greece, settled in an area stretching from north-eastern Greece to the Danube River and the Black Sea. Later, the southern part of this area was called Thrace.
Tiryns was one of the Mycenaean towns. Interesting frescoes and a Hittite figurine have been found there.
Trojan War. According to HOMER, Troy was ruled by King Priam, whose son Paris fell in love with Helen, wife of Menelaus the king of Sparta. Paris either kidnapped or eloped with Helen, and took her to Troy. The whole of Greece was outraged and an alliance of Greek states organized a seaborne invasion of Troy under the leadership of King Menelaus of Sparta, King Agamemnon of Mycenae, Achilles and Ulysses (Odysseus). But after 10 years of siege the walls of Troy still held. Then Ulysses used cunning. He built a wooden horse, packed it with soldiers, and left it outside the Trojan walls. The Greeks then pretended to sail away, accepting defeat. The joyful Trojans came out of their city and dragged the curious 'horse' back inside their walls. That night the Greeks came silently out of the horse, opened the Trojan gates, and let their comrades in. The Greeks then massacred the Trojans, plundered their city and burned it down.
Troy, the city attacked in the Trojan war, lay on the north-eastern coast of Asia Minor, near the entrance to the Dardanelles. SCHLIEMANN

Bronze miniature of Zeus

began excavations in 1871, which led to the discovery of 9 cities, each built upon the ruins of its predecessors. His belief that Homer's Troy was more than just an imaginary city was finally proved correct.

Z Zeus, the sky-god, fathered both gods and men. Well established as chief god in the Aegean civilization, he retained this role among the Greeks of later times. The Romans kept him, but called him Jupiter.

Babylon, with its exotic Hanging Gardens and its ominous Tower of Babel, was the
capital of an empire which spanned 1,500 years, situated in a desert where two rivers
meet. It was a haven for prophets, astrologers and scientists.

The Babylonians

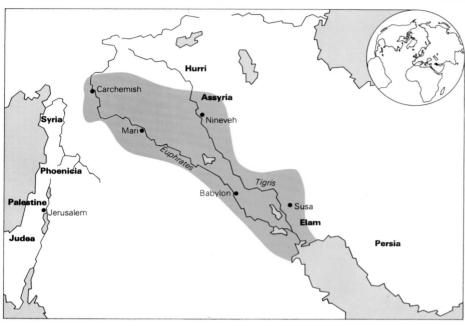

Above: Hammurabi's
empire centred on
Mesopotamia, the land
around the Euphrates and
Tigris Rivers. It extended
from Sumer into Syria.

The Semitic-speaking Amorites established their
civilization around the capital of Babylon about
1900 BC. Unlike the Sumerians, who had to
develop civilization from the beginnings, the
Amorites inherited the cultural experience of
their predecessors. They founded two Babylonian empires separated by 95 years of occupation
by their northern neighbours, the Assyrians.
Babylonia reached the peak of its influence and
expansion under King Hammurabi (reigned
1792–c.1750 BC).

Babylon was a desert city, standing on the life-
giving Euphrates River at the point where it
curved within 12 kilometres of the Tigris River.
A thousand years after Hammurabi, Babylon
was famous for its HANGING GARDENS, which
became one of the wonders of the ancient world.
Babylonian priest-scientists studied ASTROLOGY
and continued and extended the number systems
of the Sumerians.

Above: Hammurabi,
Babylon's lawyer-king,
kneels in prayer.

Babylonian society

Below the king, four main classes lived in
Babylon: the nobles, the middle class, low-
ranking freemen, and slaves. Slaves were allowed
to marry free people, and the children of such
marriages became free on the death of the slave
parent. Yet the status of slaves was far from
clear. While one set of laws treated them as
people with rights, other laws defined them as no
more than possessions of other people.

Babylon and other Amorite cities throbbed
with the bustle of workmen and traders. The
bricklayers, carpenters, butchers, cooks, brewers,
bakers, potters, metalsmiths, masons, spinners
and weavers plied their trades as they had done
in pre-Amorite times.

Under Amorite kings such as Hammurabi,
private enterprise boomed — good reason
perhaps for the spate of laws governing contracts
and dealings. A vigorous trade developed in
slaves, cattle, grain, offices of profit such as
priesthoods, loans, deposits, leases, and the
hiring of labour and property. Money lenders
thrived as the demand for business capital grew.
Some of the Babylonian deities were worshipped
as gods of commerce who welcomed the use of
their temples as trading centres. However, the
state also traded through officials called *tamkaru*,
who combined the functions of merchants,
bankers and government agents generally.

Ordinary people's houses were thick-walled
and made of mud, often semi-detached. They
were frequently built to suit the site, even at the
expense of the inhabitants' needs. Better houses,
of baked brick, were of two or more stories built
around a central courtyard.

Public buildings in Babylon were much more
ambitious architecturally than the private dwel-
lings. During the second Babylonian empire
(625-538 BC) Babylon was rebuilt on a vast scale
by King NEBUCHADNEZZAR II. The outer wall (24

Above: Mythical animals portrayed on glazed brick once adorned the Ishtar Gate of Babylon's great wall.

metres thick) had a perimeter of 18 kilometres and enclosed a city of 200,000 people. There was a road on top of the wall wide enough for a chariot to turn on. The inner wall had eight impressive gates, each sacred to a different deity. The ISHTAR gate stood over ten metres, with towers twice as high. The gateway was surfaced with glazed blue bricks cemented in bitumen. These were also decorated with magnificent reliefs of bulls, dragons and symbols of the chief god, MARDUK.

The Hanging Gardens overlooked the Ishtar gate. These were probably terraces of earth planted with trees and flowers on a huge step pyramid. Pumps raised water to the terraces through which footpaths led to the top. A road ran from the Ishtar gate to the biggest of all the Mesopotamian ziggurats which another people — the Jews — called the TOWER OF BABEL.

Below: The ziggurat of Babylon rose higher than all its predecessors. The Jews, who helped to build it during the 'Babylonian captivity', thought their taskmasters were trying to reach heaven. Toiling alongside many enslaved peoples speaking different languages, the Jews thought God had confused the workers' tongues so as to make co-operation impossible.

Above and right: Babylon, located on a branch of the Euphrates where it came near to the Tigris, was the hub of the river traffic between the Persian Gulf and the Syrian and Hittite territories to the north.

agriculture depended upon better irrigation. The transference of the centre of civilization in Mesopotamia from the delta region (Sumer) to the plain (Babylon) was a consequence of improved irrigation through the construction of canals.

Carchemish became the eastern capital of the Hittites when they were already in decline. When the Assyrians took Carchemish in 717 BC, Hittite power finally disintegrated.

Chaldeans, a Semitic people, settled in southern Mesopotamia about 1000 BC.

Their name became associated with the pursuit of astrology. After an unsuccessful attempt, they eventually seized control of Babylon in 626 BC and founded the second Babylonian empire. This fell to the Persians in 539 BC.

Cyrus the Persian rose from obscurity to found the powerful Persian empire. He overthrew the king of Media (sited in present-day Iran) about the 550s BC and conquered several other kingdoms. Babylon eventually fell to him in 539 BC and he ruled for 10 years.

D **Dreams,** now believed to be a key to understanding the unconscious mind, were in ancient times thought to reveal the future.

Clay printing matrix

One of the most famous dreams of all times was that of the pharaoh who dreamed that 7 thin cows ate 7 fat ones. Joseph the Hebrew told him that this meant 7 years of good harvests would be followed by 7 years of famine. In Babylon, *sha'ilu* priests had the special function of interpreting dreams. In theory, the priests took the puzzling dreams to a god who interpreted them for the priests to relate.

E **Ea,** Babylonian god of the waters, was also city god of Eridu. He was supposedly the father of MARDUK.

Boxers in clay c. 200s BC

Religion

Civilizations from India to the Aegean (and later to Rome and northern Europe) regularly 'borrowed' gods from one another. According to the Babylonian myth of creation, all things began with the fusion of sweet water with salt water. First came the deities. These included ANU (the powerful) and EA (of great intellect). The goddess TIAMAT personified the sea. Using storms and terrifying winds, the supergod Marduk killed Tiamat, became supreme, and brought order out of chaos. To each subordinate deity Marduk assigned a special role.

Astrology and astronomy

The Babylonians saw the world as a place subject to the whims of the gods. However, it was possible from omens, DREAMS, the movements of animals or unusual births, to foresee what the gods would do. Above all, the key lay in astrology. Priests first used astrology in Babylon to predict affairs of state such as harvests, floods, invasions and the king's life-span. Priestly records tell us: 'If the sun stands in the path of the moon, the king will be secure on the throne,' and 'If in the month of Ab the thunder god casts his mouth, there will be gloom in the land.' The need to be reasonably correct in their predictions must have spurred the priests to the study of more reliable sciences. Only late in Babylon's history did astrologers cast personal HORO-SCOPES.

Alongside the astrologers were the astronomers, and from Babylon came the oldest-known astronomical instrument, the ASTROLABE. Astronomers also recorded eclipses of the sun and the moon. There was generally a great interest in numbers. A decimal system coexisted with

F **Fabulous beasts** and monsters were common themes in the world of the ancient Middle East and eastern Mediterranean. Egypt had its sphinx and Crete its minotaur. Genii (who appear in the *Arabian Nights*) were already present in Babylon, as was the dragon, which later made its way to China. Assyria had its human-headed, winged bulls.

G **Ghee** (clarified butter), commonly used in India and nearby countries, was part of the diet of Babylon. Butter is melted or boiled to evaporate the water and to strain or skim off the solid matter. The oil of the butter which remains is the ghee. The Babylonians used it for cooking and also for various medicinal and religious purposes.

Gods were 'borrowed' from other civilizations, although the deity so taken was often given another name. MARDUK, the city god, can be equated with Zeus and Jupiter. ISHTAR, goddess of love, is equivalent to Aphrodite of the Greeks and Venus of the Romans.

H **Hanging Gardens** of Babylon were reputed to be so splendid that they were included among the Greeks' 'Seven Wonders of the World'. Remains of them have been found near the

Ea, the god of water, as judge

palace. Terraces of deep earth were supported on an arched structure, probably part of a vast step pyramid. **Horoscopes** could only be cast when knowledge was available about which planets and stars were visible at the time of a person's birth. Horoscopic astrology therefore had to await the compilation of the zodiac. Although horoscopes were cast in Egypt and Greece, they were almost certainly first cast by the CHALDEANS.

Hurrians, a little-known people, played an important role in Middle Eastern history during the 1000s BC. They probably came from the Zagros mountains of Persia. They were known to the Sumerians before 2000 BC and probably dominated Assyria during the time of

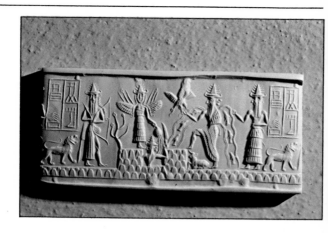

Left: Hammurabi stands before the sun god to receive the symbols of justice. Below the picture, the king's laws – the most advanced legal code up to that time – were set out in cuneiform writing on the 223-cm high basalt stele. Hammurabi's code gave rough justice with a fine touch of class distinction in its penalties.

Above: On a cylinder seal impression, the sun god Shamesh rises between 2 mountains. Ea, god of the waters, stands to the right facing Ishtar, goddess of love and fertility.

another system based on 60, and its subdivision 12. The Babylonians divided the day into 12 *roms* (each equivalent to two hours). The *rom* was subdivided into minutes, and again into seconds. A cuneiform system of symbols represented numbers up to 59 and these could be added to the symbol that represented 60.

Agriculture

Under Hammurabi a vigorous policy of CANAL BUILDING was undertaken to bring prosperity through increased agricultural yields. The staple diet was barley, which was eaten in the form of unleavened bread and drunk as beer. Other cereals eaten as bread or as a kind of porridge, included millet, wheat, rye and (after about 1000 BC) rice. Cereals were also cooked with honey, milk, GHEE, sesame oil or fruits and made into

cakes and biscuits.

Vegetables included onions, beans, peas, lentils, cucumbers, cabbages and LETTUCES; and there were fruits such as apples, apricots, figs, quinces and pomegranates. Above all, there was the date, sometimes made into date wine. Grape wine was also drunk. Added to this fairly varied diet were the products of cows, sheep and goats, whose meat was eaten at festivals.

Holidays

Religious festivals provided the occasion for holidays. These could occupy several days in a month, but there was no weekly day off such as a sabbath. The new year festival lasted from 11 to 15 days. Letters from the second Babylonian empire refer to men complaining about overwork. There is also the hint of a threatened strike: 'The people are not agreeable (to the terms of their task) and will not do the king's work.' However, there was very little democracy in Babylonia.

Language and the arts

The language of Babylonia and its northern neighbour Assyria was Akkadian, and had many forms of local dialect. Akkadian took its system of writing from Sumerian, the world's oldest written language. They were both written in cuneiform on clay tablets. Sumerian works such as the EPIC OF GILGAMESH (*see page 12*) were edited and re-arranged into new forms and Babylonia's own early *Epic of Creation* told how Marduk killed Tiamat and created the world from her body.

Surviving visual arts from Babylonia include a few statues, notably a diorite bearded head,

Below: A boundary stone records the gift of some land in southern Babylonia to Gula-Eves by the local governor. Carved symbols represent the gods invoked to protect the transaction.

Hammurabi. Their heartland in northern Mesopotamia was called Hurri. They had their own religion but their deities included Teshub (the Hittite storm god) and his wife, Hebat. Some Hittite queens had Hurrian names.

I **Ishtar** (or Astarte) was the Babylonian goddess of love, fertility and nature. In mythology she descended into Hades (hell) to search for and bring back to life her slain lover, Tammuz. This myth is believed to symbolize the re-emergence of plant life in spring, following

its 'death' in winter.

J **Judea**, a state in southern Palestine, was named after the tribe of Judah from which came the word *Jew*. Its capital, Jerusalem, was sacked in 586 BC. The state survived until AD 70, when the Romans ended it.

K **Kassites**, probably an Indo-European people, moved westwards from the mountains of Persia. They took Babylon and ruled from there between the 1700s and 1100s BC, when they re-

turned to the Persian mountains. They spoke their own language but did not write it. Their gods were probably related to those of the Persians and Hindus. After their return to Persia they survived as a distinct people for another 1,000 years, but little is known of them.

L **Lettuces** have been cultivated from earliest-known times. They are not found anywhere in the wild state. They were part of the diet of the Babylonians and probably transmitted several waterborne diseases.

M **Marduk** (or Merodach), city god of Babylon, grew in status in step with his city and became supreme god. Hymns composed in his honour are among the noblest pieces in Babylonian literature.

Mursilis I, king of the Hittites, attacked the Kassite rulers of Babylon about 1530 BC. The Hittites claimed that they destroyed Babylon and subdued the HURRIANS, but this is doubtful. Mursilis was assassinated upon his return to the homeland.

N **Nabonidus** (reigned 556- 539 BC), last king of Babylon, may have been a usurper. He was so preoccupied with religious matters that he left the state unde-

Lion c. 1000s BC

probably of Hammurabi, which was found at Susa in Elam. Examples of painting, which tended to follow Sumerian styles, can be found on the walls of Mari on the Euphrates. During the second Babylonian empire, wall motifs such as those on the Ishtar gate were typical and FABULOUS BEASTS and all kinds of monsters abounded.

Law and government

Among Babylon's greatest achievements was Hammurabi's code of laws. This laid down that wrongdoers should be judged and punished by society rather than by the victim or his family. Under the code, a man with a chronically sick wife could remarry if he undertook to continue to support his sick wife. But a debtor could enslave his wife to the man he owed money to for up to three years. If a man divorced his wife without her giving cause, he had to pay her compensation. On the death of a father, all sons inherited equally.

The code dispensed rough justice, but not equally between the classes. For example, if a doctor treated a noble who consequently lost an eye, the doctor's hands were amputated. If the doctor caused the loss of a poor freeman's eye he had to pay 50 SHEKELS of silver as compensation. When a doctor blinded a slave's eye he had to pay half the value of the slave to his or her owner. All killing was punished as murder and courts made no distinction between premeditated murder, manslaughter or accidental death.

If Hammurabi's code was heavy-handed, it was at least every man's right rather than a privilege granted to the few. Courts tried to be fair to the accused, who were allowed up to six months in which to produce witnesses. In Hammurabi the Babylonians had a conscientious king heading an efficient government.

The first Babylonian empire

Under Hammurabi (1792-1750 BC) Babylonia expanded its frontiers to include SYRIA in the west, Assyria in the north, and Elam to the east. Hammurabi deposed local princes and organized the empire into provinces under governors responsible to him. The more Babylonia prospered, the more its desert neighbours envied its wealth.

The frontiers, which had few natural defences,

Above: The Babylonians used sheep's livers in divination. This clay model shows how they were divided into 55 sections and inscribed with omens and magical formulae.

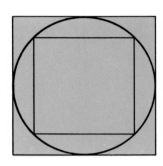

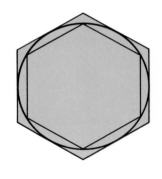

Above: Babylonian mathematicians discovered how to find the approximate area of a circle. They constructed either squares or hexagons to touch inside and outside the circle, then took half the combined areas of the inner and outer figures.

proved difficult to defend and large parts of the empire broke away under Hammurabi's successors. The KASSITES, a hill people from the northwest, took Babylon and ruled the remains of the empire for over 500 years. About 1530 BC, King MURSILIS I of the Hittites raided Babylon in force, beginning a long series of attacks by foreign armies. Another people, the HURRIANS, attacked Babylon from east of the Tigris. Generally, little is known about Babylonia during the thousand years that followed Hammurabi's rule.

The Assyrian occupation

Nabu-nasir, puppet-king of Babylon ruled without interference from Assyria, because he pursued pro-Assyrian policies. At his death in 734 BC, his kingdom of Babylon had declined into a vassal state of Assyria. South of Babylon, the CHALDEANS (supposedly subject to Babylonia) had controlled the land for about 100 years. They now openly rebelled and seized the throne. The Babylonians then sought the aid of their Assyrian overlords, who drove off the Chaldeans. But the Babylonians paid a heavy price, for in 721 BC the remains of Babylonia passed under Assyrian rule.

The second Babylonian empire

When Assyria's power declined, the Chaldeans at last took Babylon and in 625 BC they set up the second Babylonian empire under King NABOPOLASSAR. The star-studying Chaldeans were to rule Babylonia for 87 brilliant years. Nabopolassar's son, soon to become Nebuchadnezzar II (reigned 605-562 BC) fought the battle of CARCHEMISH in 605 BC. There he defeated the remnant of the Assyrian army together with the army of King NECHO of Egypt, which fled back home in disarray.

Soon, Nebuchadnezzar's empire extended from Elam to the borders of Egypt. It included Syria and PALESTINE. The Jewish kingdom of JUDEA submitted to Nebuchadnezzar, but later unwisely sided with Egypt against him. He sacked their capital of Jerusalem in 586 BC and deported the population to Babylon – a period in their history known as the BABYLONIAN CAPTIVITY. Deliverance came in 539 BC, when CYRUS THE PERSIAN defeated the Babylonian army of King NABONIDUS. Babylonia collapsed and was absorbed into the new Persian empire.

Clay man and dog c. 2000s BC

The Hittites were a warlike tribe about whom very little is known. Their iron swords and strict code of law dominated the Middle East for 300 years.

The Hittites

At about the time of Hammurabi (*see pages 33-37*), the Hittites, an Indo-Aryan people who came from the north, across the Caucasus Mountains, were establishing themselves in ANATOLIA, north-west of Babylonia. Their land had a harsher climate than Mesopotamia — more like that of the Russian steppe. Winter brought biting winds and heavy snow, but the summer sun scorched vegetation. The Hittites settled in the milder river valleys. They unified the isolated city communities of Anatolia and imposed their own system of order on them.

By about 1600 BC the Hittites had set up their capital at HATTUSAS. Soon after, they conquered northern Syria and raided Babylon. Few armies could withstand the Hittite onslaught because they fought with weapons that no one else could match — iron swords. Although the Hittites dominated the Middle East between 1500 and 1200 BC, we know little about them.

Social and economic life

The Hittites developed a code of laws similar to Hammurabi's, but it was less harsh, and the death penalty was imposed less frequently. The Hittites paid more attention to putting matters right after an offence and placed less emphasis on punishment.

Hittite kings commanded the army and were chief judges and high priests. After death and CREMATION, they were worshipped as gods. Yet while the early kings had constantly to guard their positions against jealous nobles seeking to usurp the throne, Hittite queens had a degree of power and importance rare in the ancient world. Nobles and officials of the Hittite empire belonged to a small CASTE of people related to the kings. Ordinary people — farmers, craftsmen and the like — probably descended from a native conquered people, the Hattians. The line between freemen and slaves was not clear-cut.

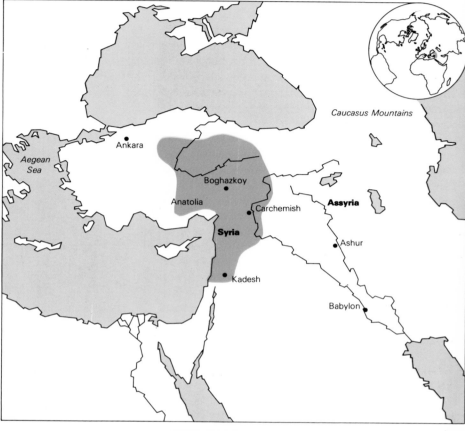

Above: The Hittite empire, centred on Anatolia, flourished from 1500 to 1200 BC with its capital at Hattusas (Boghazkoy). The map shows important places in Hittite times, including Carchemish, the later capital.

Right: The Hittite bas-relief shows a hunting scene. Skilled in war, the Hittites also excelled in hunting.

Reference

A Aegean peoples who invaded and destroyed the Hittite empire about 1200 BC, were called 'Peoples of the Sea' by the Egyptians. They included especially Mysians and Phrygians. The Phrygians later established an empire in western Anatolia. This was overthrown about 700 BC by the CIMMERIANS.
Anatolia, a mountainous peninsula, forms the Asian part of present-day Turkey.

The name came from a Greek word meaning 'sunrise'. Its other name was Asia Minor.

C Carchemish was an independent city-state in the 1400s BC which King Suppiluliumas added to the Hittite empire in the 1300s BC. It was the leading city of the weak Hittite states after Hattusas fell, but it was probably controlled by the 'Peoples of the Sea'. It fell to Assyria in 717 BC.
Caste is an hereditary class that no one can leave or enter. The Hittite ruling caste

is believed to have descended from relatives of kings.
Cimmerians were first referred to by HOMER (*see page 29*) in the *Odyssey*. He said that they lived in fog and darkness on the edge of the inhabited world. They may have been driven from south-west Russia through the Caucasus Mountains into south-western Asia by the SCYTHIANS. The Cimmerians earned a reputation for plundering.
Cremation was the method of disposing of the bodies of dead Hittite kings and queens. Funeral rites lasted about 13 days, although the body was burned by the second day. Women extinguished the fire with beer,

wine and *walhi* (a ritual drink). Then they collected the bones, soaked them in fine oil, and laid them on linen on a chair.

Hittite goddess

Bull rhyton

Religion and the arts

The stormy climate of Anatolia gave rise to the Weather god, who took many forms. In mythology, the Weather god was beaten in combat by an evil dragon. Later, with the help of the goddess Inaras and a human, the Weather god slew his enemy. The Hittites shared with the HURRIANS (*see page 35*) the storm god Teshub, his wife Hebat, and the winged goddess Shaushka.

The *cella* (holiest part of Hittite temples), was approached through two small rooms. The Weather god stood at the end of the dark cella, brilliantly lit by the light of two windows, one either side of him.

The art of the Hittites was less refined than that of their neighbours and featured crudely carved stone lions. Hattusas contained cuneiform writing in several LANGUAGES. The Hittites also used HIEROGLYPHICS.

Iron in peace and war

Hittite farmers had the advantage of iron ploughshares in tilling their thin but fertile soil. Staple crops included barley and EMMER WHEAT, vines and olives. Although bronze was by far the most common metal, the Hittites became the great ironmasters, capable of defeating most enemies. Their standing army probably included foreign mercenaries and units supplied by vassals of the king. The speedy Hittite horse-drawn war chariots carried three soldiers, while the Egyptians carried two.

History

The Hittites arrived in Anatolia about 2000 BC. They conquered the Hattians, absorbed the Hurrians, and spread throughout Anatolia and northern Syria. About 1530 BC, King MURSILIS I (*see page 36*) sacked Babylon. In 1285 BC, King MUTWATALLIS fought the indecisive battle of Kadesh against Pharaoh RAMESES II (*see page 22*). Soon after this, danger flared in the western empire. Vassal kingdoms revolted and AEGEAN PEOPLES (fleeing from the rising power of the Greeks) invaded by land and sea. About 1200 BC they burned Hattusas and Hittite power waned. CARCHEMISH became the eastern capital of a federation of weak Hittite states that survived for another 500 years. In 717 BC, Carchemish fell to new warlords, the Assyrians. Soon, the Hittites disappeared as a distinct people.

Below right: The Hittites, a warlike people from the harsher climate of the north, imposed their own rule on the small city-states of Anatolia. A Hittite soldier stands guard with his iron-tipped spear as a mounted officer approaches.

E Emmer wheat, an inferior but hardy cereal, was grown by the Hittites to produce flour and a form of beer.

H Hattusas, the Hittite capital, stood near modern Boghazköy (east of Ankara). Annitas, an early Hittite king, destroyed an earlier settlement there and put the Weather god's curse on anyone who should try to rebuild it. But another king rebuilt it about 1800 BC. About 1200 BC, the 'Peoples of the Sea', the AEGEAN PEOPLES, set it afire.

Hieroglyphics were used by the later Hittites and the inscriptions that have survived were carved on rock or stone monuments. A number of seals and 7 letters written on rolls of lead have also been excavated in Ashur (the old Assyrian capital). Hittite hieroglyphics were deciphered only in AD 1947.

L Languages of the Hittites numbered 8. Hittite and Akkadian were official languages. Hurrian was also used in some documents. Hattian, Luwian and Palaic were sometimes used by priests. Sumerian was studied as a dead language and the Mitannian language was used occasionally. The

Hittite hieroglyphics

Hittites also used hieroglyphics.

M Mitanni, a Hurrian people, became for a time the dominant people of western Asia. They drove the Egyptians out of northern Syria during the time of Pharaoh Amenophis II (reigned 1450–1425 BC). King Suppiluliumas of the Hittites (reigned 1380–1340 BC) conquered them.
Mutwatallis (King) fought Rameses II at Kadesh in 1285 BC. While fighting in Syria he gave his brother, Hattusilis, large territories to govern.

Later, Hattusilis became powerful enough to depose Mutwatallis's son and seize the throne.

S Scythians, a central Asian people, moved into southern Russia about 700 BC and formed a little-known empire. They probably retreated from central Asia because of Chinese pressure on the Hsiung-nu, nomadic Mongols who raided China. The Chinese pressurized the Hsiung-nu, who pushed the Scythians against the CIMMERIANS.

The Phoenicians, called the 'blood-red men' by those who feared them, were the greatest mariners of their time. Their cunning made them excellent pirates, mercenaries and merchants, and their intelligence shaped our present-day alphabet.

The Phoenicians

Sometime after 3000 BC a people known in the Bible as the CANAANITES moved into the narrow coastal strip between Anatolia and PALESTINE. More than any other people they were merchants and sea-going traders. We know them by their Greek name, Phoenicians. Their land was fertile but tiny, and great powers blocked territorial expansion. But the sea was rich in fish, and the Phoenicians first put to sea to feed an expanding population. Their prosperity lay in the waters that surrounded their lands.

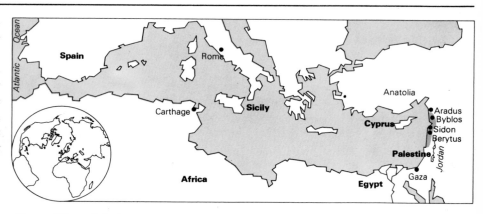

Above: Although their own land was small, Phoenician seamen and colonizers dominated the Mediterranean sea routes. Their ships sailed as far north as Britain and south to Africa, opening up new trade routes and establishing colonies along the Mediterranean coast. Settlements were founded in Carthage, Cadiz, Ibiza, Cyprus and Rhodes.

Above: The cedars of Lebanon, now few in number, once supplied timber for the navies and merchant fleets of the great powers of the Middle East. According to the Bible, 80,000 men took several years to cut and shape cedar wood for King Solomon's temple.

Reference

A Africa's boundaries were not clearly defined and no people in ancient times knew the full extent of the continent. To the Romans, Africa was that north-western part of the continent under the control of Carthage which later became a Roman province of Africa.
Alphabet was first developed in the Middle East about 1600 BC. The earliest known alphabet is called the North Semitic and several peoples contributed to its invention. Two other alphabets stemmed from it: the Aramaic, and the Canaanite which was developed by the Phoenicians. Almost all present-day alphabets are derived from the Phoenician. The Greeks added vowels to the all-consonant letters of the Phoenician alphabet, while the Romans gave it the form used in this book. Hebrew and Arabic derive from the Aramaic system.

B Ba'alat, the 'Lady of Byblos', had cow horns like the Egyptian goddess Hathor. The integration of these 2 goddesses indicated the close relationship between Byblos and Egypt.

Phoenician ivory (Syrian style)

Baal Hammon and the goddess Tanit were the chief deities of Carthage. Baal Hammon, 'lord of the altars of incense', was the Carthaginian form of the god EL. Tanit, the Carthaginian 'earth mother', became even more important than Baal Hammon by the 400s BC. This was probably because Carthage had by then an agricultural hinterland and needed a goddess of fertility.
Britain was probably visited in the 1100s BC by Phoenician traders in search of tin. They were able to make such a voyage because they navi-gated by the Pole star, which is still called the 'Phoenician star' by the Greeks.
Byblos, one of the world's oldest inhabited towns, was

Phoenician ship

The Phoenicians were the greatest mariners of their time and their ships visited every part of the Mediterranean coast and probably sailed north into the Atlantic as far as the 'tin isles' of BRITAIN, and south to the western coast of AFRICA. The Phoenician homeland possessed good natural harbours, which they developed into fortified city-state ports. Their leading bases were SIDON and TYRE, and other ports included BYBLOS, Berytus (Beirut) and Aradus (Ruad).

The name PHOENICIA may have come from the Greek word *phoinos* (blood red). The Greeks would have had two good reasons for calling the Canaanite sailors 'red men'. One was their ruddy, seafaring complexions. The other was that the clothing and skin of the seamen often bore traces of the red-purple dye known as 'Tyrian purple'. This dye — highly prized by the rich throughout the ancient world — was obtained from a shell fish called *murex* and produced by secret processes in Sidon and Tyre.

The murex secreted the dye only when dead and decaying, so the smell from Sidon and Tyre must have been sickening.

The free enterprise society

Phoenicia never unified. It was a group of allied but independent city-states ruled by merchant-kings who avoided war on land but pursued piracy at sea. If trade declined because of war, Phoenician sailors hired themselves out as shippers or MERCENARIES. No warrior king or heavy-handed central government oppressed the Phoenicians and freebooting and free enterprise were the life blood of their culture, their prime exports being cedar and pinewood.

None rivalled the Phoenicians at business; many envied them. They developed a speedy alphabetical script to keep business records and accounts and designed their cities as fortified business centres instead of trying to rival the splendours of Egypt and Babylonia.

Left: Phoenician 'roundships' lie beached while dockers of the time unload jars, sacks, timber and other exports. Pack mules, once loaded, will carry special goods direct to the importer. The Phoenicians thrived on trade; they exported purple cloth, glassware, and a whole range of goods manufactured from imported materials. Above all, they shipped their 'cedars from the Lebanon' impartially to all those who could afford to pay for them, whether for peaceful or warlike purposes.

leading trading centre of Phoenicia. Egyptian papyrus was exported to the Greeks through the port of Byblos, so papyrus became known as *byblos*. The name *Bible* (*Byblos book* or *papyrus book*) comes from Byblos.

C Canaan probably meant 'Land of the Purple' (the Tyrian purple). It originally comprised only the coastal strip north of present-day Haifa, but in time its borders changed. In the Old Testament and to the Egyptians, it covered all Palestine including Gaza and

the eastern bank of Jordan. **Canaanites** included Phoenicians and, loosely, other peoples occupying the land known as Palestine. The southern Canaanites were conquered by the Hebrews, Aramaeans and PHILISTINES.

D Dido is said to have gained the site of Carthage by a trick – only to be expected of the daughter of a Phoenician merchant-king. She bought a piece of hill-side 'as big as an ox-hide could cover', and then, cunningly, she cut the hide into thin strips and joined them

end to end to form a circle around the base of the hill. Then she claimed the hill as her territory under the terms of the bargain.

E El, the great god of Canaan, was believed to make the rivers flow into the seas and so ensure the fertility of the earth. He was 'father of the gods' — especially of Baal.

G Glass was in use in the Middle East from about 2500 BC. The earliest known glass objects are a green rod from Babylon and some

beads from Egypt. About 1500 BC, the Phoenicians were famed as makers of glass vessels and they probably invented the technique

Bronze warrior

of glassblowing between 300 and 100 BC.

M Mercenaries, soldiers (and occasionally sailors) who fought for money irrespective of national loyalties, were common in the ancient times. David, who in the Old Testament slew Goliath and eventually became king of Israel, was probably a mercenary.

P Palestine (Philistia, land of the Philistines) was the name given by the Greeks about 500-400 BC to

Religion

Phoenician deities were closely connected with those of neighbouring countries. Many were nature gods. BA'ALAT, the 'Lady of Byblos', resembled the Egyptian goddess Hathor. Another deity of Byblos, RA, was akin to his Egyptian namesake. EL, the great god of all Canaan, ensured the fertility of the land although he lived by the sea. His rival was an even greater god, Baal. The word *Baal* in Semitic languages had a generalized meaning and there were as many Baals as there were religious centres. Baal worship was especially repugnant to the Hebrews who settled in southern CANAAN (the 'Land of the Purple').

Language and artistic craftwork

About 1600 BC the Phoenicians realized that all languages used no more than about 30 sounds. For each of 22 sounds they drew a symbol or

Below left: Fertility goddesses figured prominently in the religion of the Phoenicians and their neighbours. Taken to Carthage, the Phoenician religion became barbarously bloodthirsty.

Above: The shekel, originally a piece of gold or silver weighing about 14 g that circulated as money, later became a coin. A shekel of late Phoenician times

shows (*left*) an owl in the stereotyped Egyptian style and (*right*) a dolphin together with the murex from which came the 'Tyrian purple' dye.

letter. These 22 letters formed the first ALPHABET. Since then, most of the world (excluding China and Japan) has developed alphabetic languages derived from the Phoenician.

The arts and crafts of Phoenicia had a commercial base. Imported ivory, gold, silver, ebony, silk and precious stones were deftly worked into luxuries for export. Phoenician manufactured exports included jewellery, Tyrian purple cloth, fine linen, furniture, embroideries, metalwork, faience and GLASS. The Phoenicians were possibly the main inventors of glass and the technique of glassblowing.

History of Phoenicia

The Phoenicians developed their city-states over a long period of time (2900–1500 BC). They stood at the crossroads of several great powers and usually had to acknowledge the overlordship of one or more of them. The struggles between the Hittites and the Egyptians especially threatened their welfare and by the 1300s BC, the Phoenician cities found it expedient to divide their loyalties between the two great powers.

When Egypt's power waned (about 920 BC) the Phoenician cities began a period of real independence lasting about two generations, but in 868 BC a new military power, Assyria, advanced into the Mediterranean and forced the Phoenicians to pay tribute. When Assyria fell in 612 BC, Phoenicia became a pawn in a power

the coastal regions between Sinai in Egypt and northern Syria.
Philistines were natives of Philistia (Palestine). They used iron tools and weapons which made them more powerful than the CANAANITES and Hebrews. The clash between the Israelites (northern Hebrews) and the Philistines is symbolized in the Bible by the fight between David and Goliath.
Phoenicia covered roughly the area of modern Lebanon and adjacent areas of Syria and Israel. It is not known what name the Phoenicians

gave to themselves and their country. Possibly they used the terms Canaanites and Canaan. The name Phoenician probably came from the Egyptian *Fenkhw*, meaning an Asian. This became *Phoinikes* in Greek, which could also mean 'red men'.
Punic Wars were fought from 264-241, 218-201, and 149-146 BC. In each war Rome defeated Carthage. Hamilcar Barca commanded the Carthaginians in Sicily in the first war and his son, Hannibal, commanded all Carthaginian forces in the second war. In the third and

final war, Rome showed no mercy. The few citizens of Carthage who survived were sold into slavery and Carthage was totally destroyed.

'Mona Lisa' of Nimrud

The Punic Wars are an important stage in the history of Rome.

R **Ra** of Foreign Lands, and Ra who is on Pharaoh's Lake, were 2 Phoenician forms of the great god Ra, borrowed from Egypt.
Rome rose to supremacy in Mediterranean Europe after the decline of Greece and Macedonia. For more than 200 years its great rival was Carthage, which it finally destroyed in 146 BC.

S **Sacrifice** of human beings to the gods was

an annual event in Carthage. Evidence suggests that sacrifices of boys from leading families were made to BAAL HAMMON and to Tanit. Such sacrifices had once been usual among the Phoenicians and the Israelites. The peoples of Canaan generally thought that the 'first fruits' (including the first-born children) should be offered to the gods. Carthaginian human sacrifice was particularly abhorrent because it continued long after others had abandoned it. The practice of sacrificing animals was still carried on by most

struggle between Chaldean Babylonia and Egypt. In 538 BC, Phoenicia passed under the control of Persia, but again the Phoenicians bought survival by redirecting their loyalties to the new overlords.

Carthage, the African stronghold

Assyria's bureaucratic rule was irksome to the enterprising Phoenicians and it encouraged more of them to settle in colonies abroad. According to Phoenician tradition, DIDO, a princess of Tyre, led a migration to north-west Africa in 814 BC. There, near modern Tunis, she founded New Capital, now known as Carthage. She is said to have gained the land by a trick.

As time passed, Carthage grew stronger than the homeland had ever been. The Carthaginians built an outer harbour to shelter their commercial ships and an inner harbour as a base for their warships. A tall naval tower was built on an island in the inner harbour and from its heights lookouts kept a constant watch against the approach of enemy vessels or spy ships. All ships entered the fortified harbour through a 22 metres wide gap that could be securely closed by heavy chains.

The city's 80 square kilometres was enclosed by a massive towered WALL along its 35 kilometre perimeter. The defence forces included 300 elephants, 4,000 cavalrymen with horses, and 20,000 infantrymen.

Above: Phoenician *biremes* – warships having 2 banks of oars and a single square sail – were built for speed and manoeuvrability. *Round ships* (*right*) were built for trade.

Above: This amphora-shaped sand-core glass bottle dating from the 300s BC illustrates the great skill of Phoenician glassmakers, renowned throughout the Middle East. The Phoenicians probably invented glassblowing between 300 and 100 BC.

The Carthaginian way of life

By 500 BC the city held some 200,000 people. Its African hinterland spread to take in 50,000 square kilometres and another half million people. Like their forebears, the Carthaginians continued to excel as manufacturers, traders, shippers, pirates and colonists and they added SICILY and much of SPAIN to their empire.

In changing times, the bloodthirsty Carthaginian religion was despised by other Mediterranean peoples. Uncaring, the Carthaginians continued to SACRIFICE the children of nobles to appease their horned sky god, BAAL HAMMON. Worshippers sought his favours by practising self-mutilation before him. Other Mediterranean peoples had long abandoned such practices.

The end of Carthage

The chief rivals at sea for the Phoenicians had been the Greeks. From them, the Carthaginians had little to fear. But by 348 BC a more formidable power was rising across the Mediterranean — ROME. In that year, Carthage concluded an advantageous treaty with Rome. The uneasy peace lasted for 84 years until war came between the two powers over a dispute in Sicily. The Romans fought three PUNIC WARS (Carthaginian Wars): 264-241, 218-201, and 149-146 BC. Rome's final triumph was absolute and Carthage disappeared from history and became the Roman province of Africa.

---

peoples in Carthaginian times.
Sicily was a Phoenician colony before it was infiltrated by Greek colonists. In

409 BC, a struggle for Sicily began between Greeks and Carthaginians. Later, the Carthaginians battled with the Romans for the island and by 210 BC, Rome controlled the whole of Sicily, which became its granary.
Sidon, founded before 2000 BC, developed into a prosperous city over the following 1,000 years. Although the PHILISTINES burned it in the 1100s BC, it recovered. Sidon colonized several places in the eastern Mediterranean, including Cyprus. The city's prosperity continued under the successive rule of Assy-

rians, Egyptians, Persians, Macedonians and Romans.
Spain was visited by Phoenician traders and colonists from about 600 BC. Later the Greeks founded settlements there and by 520 BC, Carthage held much of southern Spain. Carthaginian-Roman rivalry in Spain led to the second PUNIC WAR and when Carthage finally lost, Spain came under Roman influence.

T **Tyre** probably began as a colony of Sidon. It came under Egyptian control in the 1400s BC and by the

1100s BC it outmatched Sidon in importance. In 814 BC, colonists from Tyre founded Carthage. By then Tyre was caught up in the turbulent affairs of the Assyrian empire. It fell to Babylon in 573 BC, and to Persia in 538 BC. Tyre suffered terrible destruction by ALEXANDER THE GREAT (*see page 16*).

W **Wall** of Carthage stood over 12 metres high and 9 metres thick. Four-storeyed towers rose high above the wall every 60 or so metres and built into it were lower stables for elephants,

higher stables for horses, and barracks for 24,000 soldiers.

Ivory of cow suckling calf

Punic tombstone

The all-conquering Assyrians were the supreme masters of war and the most cruel race of their time. Yet their interest in culture was profound and it is largely due to them that we know so much about the ancient world today.

The Assyrians

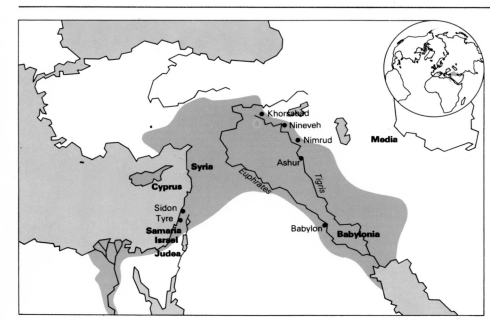

One of the great Mesopotamian civilizations, Assyria was centred on the Tigris River north of Babylon. At first its capital was ASHUR, later NINEVEH. The Assyrians had less fertile land than the Sumerians and Babylonians and consequently there was pressure on them to expand their territory as their population increased. But whenever they tried to push back their borders they were repulsed by powerful neighbours, such as the Hittites and Babylonians.

The warrior state

The Assyrians had to become a warrior people to survive, and all men were conscripted into the army. They attacked, defeated and often annexed neighbouring countries, so creating a vast empire, in the process becoming the supreme masters of the art and science of war. They excelled at siegecraft and their special techniques

Above: The map shows the empire of Assyria, which absorbed all its neighbours between about 880 and 626 BC. The Assyrians 'fell like a wolf on the fold' before they in turn finally succumbed to the Medes and Persians.

Right: Ashurnasirpal II believed that he had a divine right to hunt wild animals and employed hunting dogs to aid in these lavish pursuits.

Reference

A **Aramaeans** occupied Aram, a region of northern Syria, in 1100-700 BC, and seized areas eastwards into Mesopotamia. Assyria fought several wars against them. Tigʻath-Pileser I (reigned 1115-1077 BC) claimed to have undertaken 28 campaigns against the Aramaeans and their allies the Ahlamu. Little is known of these people, but King Ashur-resh-ishi (reigned 1133-1116) described himself as 'the one who crushes the widespread forces of the Ahlamu'.

Aramaic became the international language of the Middle East by about 1700 BC. It dominated the area for about 1,300 years, and was even the official language of the Persian empire. It was very likely the language of Jesus. Arabic replaced it after AD 622 and few Aramaic documents have survived because they were written on parchment, and were less durable than writings on clay or stone.

Ashur (or Assur), a warrior god, was the chief deity of Assyria. In the Assyrian version of the Babylonian myth of creation, Ashur replaced Marduk, the chief Babylo-

Ivory goat

nian god. Ashur's symbol was a winged circle, often enclosing a male figure wearing a 3 horned headpiece. This man (or god) sometimes held a bow. Ashur's symbol was also used by the kings of Assyria.

Ashur (or Assur), capital city of early Assyria, was occupied before 2000 BC. It was a small city, the importance of which dwindled as NINEVEH, NIMRUD and KHORSABAD rose in importance. It was finally destroyed by the Babylonians in 614 BC.

Ashurbanipal succeeded his father, ESARHADDON, to the throne of Assyria in 668 BC. According to Esarhaddon's wishes, Ashurbanipal's brother (Shamush-Shumukin) became his co-equal as

Ashurnasirpal II

included the use of speedy CHARIOTS from which archers shot arrows with deadly accuracy. Like the Hittites, they had weapons of iron, not bronze. The Assyrians have left us a permanent record of their battles carved in stone on the walls of their splendid palaces.

The Assyrians gained a reputation for CRUELTY. It was said that they skinned their victims alive, impaled or burned them to death. Possibly they themselves exaggerated the extent of their cruelty to discourage resistance, or their enemies overstated the case for propaganda purposes.

Libraries

The Assyrians were not just soldiers and they had a great respect for the culture of the peoples they conquered. When they seized a city they preserved its LIBRARY and their scribes translated the information they found there into the ASSYRIAN LANGUAGE (when necessary), so that it could be put to practical use. The library of King ASHURBANIPAL at Nineveh was particularly impressive, being arranged into sections such as mathematics, astronomy, medicine, religion and history.

Social structure and economic problems

In Assyria, all land was the king's in theory, and to a large extent in fact too. Much of it was given

Above: Assyrian astronomers used a circular clay instrument in making calculations. It was inscribed with forecasts derived from their observations of the moon.

Right: King Ashurnasirpal II, who began Assyria's conquests, relaxes from war by hunting lions. This bas-relief from Nimrud is one of many now in museums, on which the Assyrians recorded in detail their vigorous activities in war and peace. The king aims his bow carefully at a wounded lion while the charioteer whips the horses into a gallop.
Below: Deer run headlong into a trap.

by him to government officials and veteran soldiers as a reward for loyal service. But landholders had to pay TAXES. They paid a 25 per cent tax on grain, ten per cent on straw, and an unknown amount on livestock. They also had to give money to the temples and pay water transport tolls. They could buy themselves out of militia service.

Economic problems motivated some of Assyria's wars. The ARAMAEANS, a group of freebooting nomadic tribes who occupied northern Syria between 1100 and 700 BC, raided and seized large areas of Mesopotamia. When they cut the vital trade links with the Mediterranean coast, the Assyrians pushed them back and brought the whole area westwards to the Mediterranean under their control. Sidon, Tyre and other Phoenician cities became part of the Assyrian empire. Unlike the easy-going Babylonians, the Assyrians brought most of the economy of the

crown prince of Babylon. Ashurbanipal was noted for his passionate interest in Nineveh's library.
Ashurnasirpal II kept Ashur as Assyria's religious capital but for strategic purposes moved the secular capital to Nimrud (Calah). Nimrud seems to have been replaced as the capital soon afterwards by the more ancient city of Nineveh.
Assyrian language was at first a dialect of Akkadian. From about the time of TIGLATH-PILESER III it was replaced by Aramaic. This was written on parchment and

used to supplement the cuneiform script still used on clay and stone.

C **Chariots,** the chief vehicles of the ancient world, were in use in Babylon about 2000 BC, drawn by asses. The Hyksos invaders of Egypt introduced horse chariots into that country about 1700 BC. The Assyrians fitted limb-cutting scythes to the wheels of their chariots which were drawn by 3 horses and carried 1 driver and an archer trained to shoot with deadly accuracy.
Cruelty in warfare and tor-

ture after defeat were usual in the ancient world and of all the nations, Assyria's image is worst. However, the Assyrians never staged public spectacles of calcu-

Relief from the Palace of Sennacherib

lated cruelty such as the Romans delighted in. They seem to have practised cruelty more to deter resistance to their authority. One of the main complainants

against Assyria was the kingdom of Judea. Its chief resentment was not Assyria's inhumanity but its commercial success and the alleged practice of witchcraft. Despite the enmity between them, Ahaz, a king of Judea, successfully sought Assyrian aid against Israel and Syria.
Cyaxares is believed to have reigned over Media for about 40 years (c.625-c.585 BC). Little is known about him except what is told by Herodotus. This ancient Greek historian wrote that in his youth Cyaxares was de-

Below: Having decided to resist rather than surrender, those besieged by the Assyrians usually defended their city desperately, believing that defeat would bring indiscriminate and painful deaths such as flaying or impalement for the leaders, and enslavement and deportation for the survivors. However, not all vanquished enemies were badly treated, and the Assyrians often left a conquered king or governor to rule his city as before, subject to his working for Assyrian interests.

Above: An Assyrian siege tower approaches the wall of the besieged city. Assyrian engineers devised several kinds of assault machines, including battering rams.

Right: Assyrian archers shoot their deadly arrows at the defenders from behind an improvised wickerwork shield.

empire under state control and Phoenician resistance to the levying of taxes was finally put down by Assyrian troops.

Religion

The gods and religious festivals of Assyria were closely allied to those of Sumeria and Babylonia. Most Assyrian myths, too, paralleled those of Babylon. ASHUR, the city-god of the capital Ashur, became the national god of the Assyrian empire. Probably to promote loyalty from conquered peoples, Assyrian priests identified him with earlier Mesopotamian gods such as Enlil. In the time of SARGON II, Ashur became identified with Anshar, the celestial world and parent of other gods. Under SENNACHERIB, Ashur became the counterpart of MARDUK (*see page 36*).

Ashur was the religious equivalent of the Assyrian state. As god of the most warlike power in the Middle East he was given detailed written reports by the kings, outlining their military campaigns.

---

feated by a Scythian army when he laid siege to Nineveh. Cyaxares took Ashur in 614 BC and, with Nabopolassar, destroyed Nineveh in 612 BC.

Cyprus, because of its position between several great powers, early on became an important trading centre. Mycenaean traders visited the island about 1400 BC. About 800 BC it came under Phoenician rule, and in 709 BC the several kings of Cyprus submitted to SARGON II. It remained part of the Assyrian empire for about 40 years. From about 669 BC

Cyprus had over 100 years of independence before its conquest by Egypt.

E **Esarhaddon** succeeded to the throne in 680 BC after his brothers murdered his father, SENNACHERIB. The main Assyrian army prepared to oppose Esarhaddon and the army that he commanded. However, Esarhaddon's enemies became divided among themselves when they heard that the goddess Ishtar favoured him and the main army then acclaimed him. Under his brilliant generalship the As-

Esarhaddon and captives

syrian empire expanded to its greatest extent.

K **Khorsabad** was excavated in AD 1842 and 1851. Statues of SARGON II and winged bulls were found and taken to the Louvre, Paris. In 1932, archaeologists found hundreds of clay tablets at the site bearing cuneiform writings in Elamite. These included a list of kings supposed to have reigned from about 2200 to 730 BC.

L **Library** of ASHURBANIPAL at Nineveh was one of

the world's greatest collections of recorded knowledge. Present-day information about Mesopotamian science and literature comes largely from material salvaged from the ruins of the library. Records show that the Assyrians continued the scholastic work of the Sumerians and Babylonians. Alongside the scientific documents are extensive pseudo-scientific works such as the study of omens.

M **Media** lay in what is now north-western Iran. Its first known mention

When Ashur became Assyria's capital (about 1350 BC), a great period of ziggurat and temple building began. This continued until the fall of Assyria. Great monuments were built at Nineveh, NIMRUD and KHORSABAD. Like the Babylonians, the Assyrians built splendid palaces with entrances flanked by human-headed WINGED BULLS.

Assyrian art generally followed the pattern of Sumeria and Babylon and was secular rather than religious. But the reliefs that covered the walls of the palaces were essentially Assyrian and depicted lifelike details of dress and weapons, horses and chariots. The Assyrians themselves are pictured as stocky, determined and woolly-bearded and the reliefs confirm their inhumanity.

Administration of the empire

The Assyrian people represented only a fraction of the population of the empire and they had to rely heavily on foreign manpower. A high proportion of their army and their workforce was therefore non-Assyrian. Labour in the homeland was scarce considering the immense amount of building construction that was undertaken and tens of thousands of prisoners of war and exiled peoples were taken in as forced labourers. From Samaria (the capital of Israel) alone, 27,000 people were sent to Assyria as forced labourers.

Payments of tax and TRIBUTE from conquered peoples went mainly to the upkeep of the army and to the cost of building. But Assyrian rule was not without benefits. The new order brought peace and prosperity in place of the perpetual petty wars of smaller states.

Speedy communication between the chief Assyrian cities and the provinces was vital to the existence of the empire. To achieve this, the Assyrians constructed an imperial ROAD SYSTEM with relay stations and guard posts.

The status given to conquered provinces depended largely upon the degree of co-operation they gave to Assyria. Some kept their own rulers but paid tribute to Assyria. Others, although

Above: Men impaled on stakes confirm Assyrian cruelty following the capture of Lachish, near Jerusalem in Judea, about 700 BC.

Below: The heavy, metal-fitted chariots of the Assyrians carried 3 men, like the Hittite chariots. The horses were vulnerable, however, and a startled horse could overturn a chariot, causing chaos on the battlefield.

is in Assyrian documents of the 800s BC. The Median capital, Ecbatana, was on the site of present-day Hama-dan. The Median tribes probably remained disunited until about 625 BC when CYAXARES set up a single kingdom of Media.

N Nimrud was the military capital of Assyria under ASHURNASIRPAL II. This king celebrated the official opening of the city by giving a 10-day banquet for nearly 70,000 people.

Nineveh was made the capital of Assyria by SEN-NACHERIB, who transformed it into a magnificent city. It was excavated by the British archaeologist A.H.Layard in AD 1845-51. With great diffi-

Ivory furniture, Nimrud

culty he removed to the British Museum, London, a remarkable collection of bas-reliefs portraying mostly war or hunting scenes. With them went thousands of clay tablets from Ashurbanipal's library.

R Road systems in Assyria were established by TIGLATH-PILESER III. Posting stages were organized across the empire so that messages could pass quickly between the king and his provincial governors. Exit roads, surfaced with cobblestones, led out from Assyrian cities to allow for the efficient passage of the armies. Sennacherib decreed that anyone encroaching upon the 'royal road' out of Nineveh would be impaled.

S Sargon II founded the last Assyrian dynasty following a military coup. His dynasty included:
Sargon II   (r.721–705 BC)
Sennacherib   (r.704–681 BC)
Esarhaddon   (r.680–669 BC)
Ashurbanipal (r.668–626 BC)
Ashur-etillu-ili (r.c.625–623 BC)
Sin-shar-Ishkun
                     (r.622–c.612 BC)

Sennacherib, son of Sargon II, rebuilt Nineveh and made it the capital. Exasperated by persistent op-

Sargon II and an official

Above: Winged bulls with human heads guarded the gates of King Sargon II's palace at Khorsabad. The bulls had 5 legs, so that 4 could be seen from the side, 2 from the front.

Left: Flushed with success following the storming of a city that long defied them, Assyrian soldiers present the heads of captives taken after its final fall.

allowed to keep their own ruler, had an Assyrian 'adviser' at court. Some had an Assyrian governor who ruled with absolute power.

The Assyrians were the contemporaries of the Babylonians and Hittites, but their period of power began only in the 800s BC. ASHURNASIRPAL II (reigned 883-858 BC) chased the Aramaeans westwards to the Mediterranean and took the Phoenician cities. TIGLATH-PILESER III (a usurper who reigned 745-727 BC) extended the empire from the old Sumerian cities into Asia Minor. He incorporated Palestine and Syria and his armies threatened the borders of Egypt. Babylonia was left to the rule of its own kings so long as they followed Assyria's policies. When the Chaldeans tried to seize control of Babylonia, Tiglath-Pileser III finally annexed it directly to Assyria.

The Sargonid dynasty

In 721 BC, a military revolt placed Sargon II on the throne and his dynasty, too, fought perpetual wars of expansion conquering the Greek cities on CYPRUS. Sargon's son, Sennacherib (reigned 705-681 BC), defeated an alliance of Elamites, Babylonians and Chaldeans and quelled an Egyptian-inspired revolt in Judea.

Exasperated at Babylon's persistent opposition, Sennacherib devastated the splendid city, turning it into a wasteland. Even the city god Marduk was taken into captivity to Ashur. Sennacherib's sons murdered him, possibly because of his destruction of Babylon. One of them, ESARHADDON, (reigned 681-669 BC), rebuilt the city and restored Marduk to his temple.

Esarhaddon's son, Ashurbanipal (reigned 669-626 BC), was a scholar, but nevertheless, he and the two sons who followed him had to fight the same dreary cycle of wars. At this time Assyria's strength was beginning to wane and about 621 BC it came close to civil war. Nabopolassar, the Chaldean who seized the throne of Babylon in 625 BC, allied Babylon with MEDIA. Soon after, Nabopolassar and CYAXARES (the Median king) jointly attacked Assyria. Not all Assyria's vassal states wanted it to fall. They feared that if Assyria collapsed the Scythians, Cimmerians and other nomads would sweep into the Middle East and destroy civilization. But Assyria's allies could not save it and in 612 BC the Babylonians and Medes destroyed Nineveh. It was never rebuilt. In 609 BC, Assyria ceased to exist.

position which he had to face from his vassal, the king of Babylon, Sennacherib destroyed that city. He was subsequently murdered by his sons, possibly because of this.

T **Taxes** were collected by the 'lord of the city' – an agent of the Assyrian government who was often the original ruler of a conquered place. The 'lord' had a small garrison to enforce his orders. Conquered peoples often objected to paying taxes to the Assyrian government. The Assyrians taxed the merchants of conquered Sidon and Tyre on timber from the mountains that entered their warehouses. In protest, the outraged Phoenicians rioted and killed a tax collector before an Assyrian army quelled them. Inspectors enforced the payment of taxes on boats, fisheries, cattle, clipped wool, and even divorces and burials. *Tithes* (10% of the value of certain items, paid to the temple) were charged on date crops, fish catches, cattle, cornland and rents (paid in kind).

Tiglath-Pileser III came to the throne in 745 BC following a revolt in Nimrud (then the capital) where the old royal family was murdered.

Warriors with round shields

He took over when the Assyrian empire was in a state of political anarchy and near to military and economic collapse. The king's brilliant administration and military successes restored Assyrian power.

Tribute was a regular (sometimes annual) sum of money or amount of goods paid by the ruler of a subordinate state to the ruler of a more powerful one. The king paying tribute accepted the other king as his overlord or *suzerain* (usually unwillingly). In theory, payment of tribute also bought peace and protection.

W **Winged bulls** with human heads guarded the entrances of SARGON II'S palace at KHORSABAD. They wore the horned headdress of divinity and probably represented benevolent genii. Being designed to stand against walls, these massive structures had only 2 sculptured surfaces, front and side. A curious feature of the bulls is that they have 5 legs. They were so designed that, when viewed side-on, 4 legs would be visible. The bulls are now at the British Museum.

The Persians were the first race to acknowledge one invisible God and the first to spread the use of money as currency. Under their rule the Middle East enjoyed peace, prosperity and religious tolerance.

The Persians

Most civilizations come to maturity after a long period of cultural and military development, but Persia entered world history with dramatic suddenness about 547 BC. In that year CYRUS II, king of the small Iranian state of Anshan, reached the climax of his career. After 13 years of war he united the several Iranian (Aryan) kingdoms of Media and PERSIA under his leadership so that his domains extended from Asia Minor and the Black Sea to the Gulf of Oman.

The ACHAEMENID DYNASTY that Cyrus founded was to last only two centuries, but it came to rule the largest empire that the world had known up to that time. The old territories of the Sumerians, Egyptians, Indus Valley peoples, Babylonians, Hittites, Phoenicians and Assyrians, were all absorbed into the Persian empire by about 400 BC. Parts of ETHIOPIA, the Balkans and central Asia also came under Persian rule. At its height, the Persian empire was as big as present-day Europe without Russia.

The Persians originated very little; mostly they built upon the achievements of their predecessors and improved them. But the Persian peace that they imposed brought a new stability and prosperity.

Persian government

Although the Persian kings were ruthless in extending their conquests, they were not cruel by comparison with their neighbours and predecessors. Toleration rather than intimidation was the keynote of their imperial policy and the Achaemenid kings sought to assimilate conquered peoples into the empire on favourable terms. Persian rule was less rigid than Assyrian, and so less objectionable. Babylon submitted to Cyrus without a fight and many Babylonians preferred his rule to that of Nabonidus, the last Chaldean king. Instead of destroying Babylon as

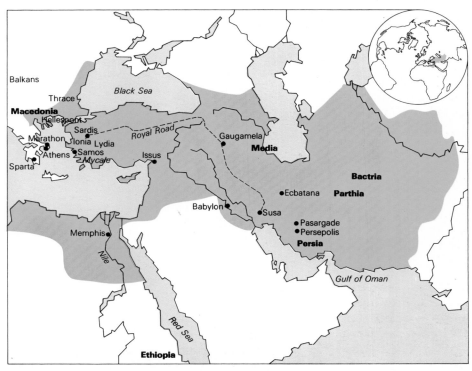

Above: The Persian empire burst suddenly into history to swallow up the territories of all previous civilizations west of China. No other empire equalled its size until Han China and Rome appeared. It fell suddenly to Alexander the Great in 334–331 BC.

Sennacherib had done, Cyrus honoured it by making the city one of his several capitals.

The Persian empire was organized into SATRAPIES (provinces) by DARIUS I (reigned 521-486 BC), the third king of Persia. Each satrapy had its *satrap* (governor). But Darius I, mindful perhaps of Cyrus's career, was suspicious of satraps who might grow too powerful and alongside each satrap was a general and also a secretary of state. With power divided between them, the three officials had to report direct to the king. His personal inspectors visited them regularly, accompanied by a troop of soldiers.

The Persians took over and extended the Assyrian road system. The Royal Road, built by Darius, ran 2,500 kilometres from SARDIS to SUSA and was used by traders as well as soldiers.

Reference

A **Achaemenid dynasty** had 11 kings, including: (dates BC)

Cyrus II (the Great) 559–530
Cambyses II 530–522
Darius I (the Great) 522–486
Xerxes I 486–465
Artaxerxes III 358–c.337
Darius III 336–c.330

Ahura-Mazda (or Ormuzd), the Supreme Creator, was believed to be engaged in a perpetual battle against the Evil God, Angra Mainyu (Ahriman). Their struggle is told in the Avesta, the Zoroastrian holy book.

Anahita (the Unspotted) was the Persian fertility goddess.

Artaxerxes III gained the throne by murdering his brother's family and continued a reign of terror until his death. His strong rule prolonged the life of the Persian empire. Finally, he was poisoned.

B **Bactrians** lived in Bactria, an eastern satrapy through which Siberian and Indian trade passed on its way to Persia. Bactria later became an independent state and annexed part of Chinese Turkestan and

Bactrian leading camel

northern India. About 130 BC, Bactria fell to the *Sakas,* a nomadic tribe.

C **Cambyses II** was regent of Babylon before reigning 530–522 BC. He invaded Egypt in 525 BC, and defeated and executed Pharaoh Psamtik III. Arab allies provided his solders with water across Sinai. Cambyses went insane, became irrationally cruel and probably committed suicide.

Croesus, the last king of Lydia, was probably killed by CYRUS II. A Greek story tells that Cyrus, relenting, tried to stop him burning on the Persian execution pyre. Supposedly, the god Apollo quenched the flames with

Early Persian pot

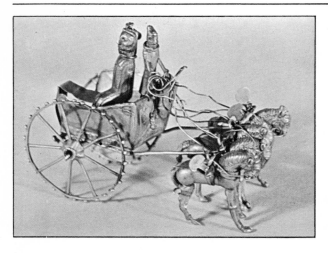

Right: This magnificent silver dish shows a man, possibly a king, killing lions. It is a fine example of Sassanian art.

Left: A gold miniature model – a masterpiece of Persian metalworking art – shows the kind of chariot used in Persia shortly before the Macedonian conquest.

Mounted couriers sped the kings' orders along the Royal Road, delivering them to the remotest borders in two weeks.

Except for Persia itself (which was privileged) all satrapies paid taxes to the central government. In previous empires taxes and tribute had been paid in kind. But now MONEY — a much more convenient form of exchange — was coming into use. Learning from CROESUS, the last king of LYDIA (defeated and annexed by Cyrus), Darius I issued a gold coin — the *daric*. Soon, this passed as currency even outside the empire. Apart from monetary taxes, each satrapy continued to send goods in kind as tribute to Persia according to its ability and Persia's need. Payments in kind from all the 20 to 30 satrapies included corn, sheep, mules, horses, hunting dogs, gold dust, children, and FRANKINCENSE and MYRRH.

Apart from the payments to the Persian court, the satrap himself exacted tribute. It is said that Darius I, having been assured that the taxes he proposed to levy could be borne, halved them. He knew that the satraps would finally double the levy to give themselves as much as the king received. However, Persia's taxes were not oppressive. Darius received every year in cash alone the equivalent of over three million gold sovereigns, but this was not excessive considering the enormous size of his empire.

The religions of the Persians
The Persian kings were not bigoted and in the satrapies the conquered peoples were free to

Far right: Archers, depicted here on glazed brick, formed the backbone of the Persian armies that created the world's largest empire then known.

Above: A gold drinking cup of the 400s BC found at Ecbatana, one of the Persian capitals, has the decorative but highly formal design typical of ancient Persian art. Skill in depicting animals was another strong feature of Persian art.

worship their own deities. But the religions of Persia were distinctly different from those of the old empires it had annexed. Three religions were practised among the Medes and Persians. These were: the kings' religion based on the one God, Ahura-Mazda, the God of gods; the people's religion centred on the god MITHRAS and the goddess ANAHITA; and the cult of the MAGI. The three religions of Persia became to some extent intermixed.

From Ahura-Mazda, creator of heaven and earth, the Persian kings supposedly drew their authority. The god had no images but was worshipped in the form of a symbol: a bearded, upright male figure centrally placed in an open wing. The religion of Ahura-Mazda was founded by ZOROASTER (Zarathustra in Persian), who may have lived about 660-583 BC or possibly much earlier. The followers of Ahura-Mazda (called ZOROASTRIANS) were among the first peoples to acknowledge only one God. He was symbolized by a bearded man on an open wing.

Mithras, later identified with the sun, had connections with the Aryan gods of India. But Mithras was also identified as an assistant to Ahura-Mazda in his fight against evil. Anahita was the Persian goddess of fertility.

The MAGI were probably a Median tribe who provided the priests and scholars of the empire: the word 'magic' comes from their cult. They were also astrologers who drew inspiration from the Chaldeans. Their chief function was to carry out a certain ritual, the nature of which is unknown.

---

rain and Croesus became Cyrus's friend.
Cyrus II the Great (c.600-529 BC) is surrounded with legends about his birth. He died probably in present-day Pakistan and was buried at Parsagade.

D **Darius I** the Great (c.558-486 BC) was a distant cousin of CAMBYSES. He gained the throne after the murder of GAUMATA (the false Prince Smerdis). He proved a most competent general and administrator. In pursuing the Scythians he began the Greco-Persian wars.

Darius I

E **Ethiopia** was traditionally founded about 1000 BC, but this cannot be confirmed. Ethiopian pharaohs ruled in Egypt's 25th dynasty (750–656 BC).

F **Frankincense and myrrh,** used medicinally and for fumigation, came from the red gum exuded by *Burseraceaea* (incense trees). They were used by the MAGI in their mysterious ceremonies.

G **Gaumata,** a Magi, impersonated Cambyses's dead brother Smerdis (Bardiya) and usurped the throne from the mad and unpopular Cambyses. He ruled briefly in 522 BC before being assassinated. A purge of the Magi followed. Supporters of Gaumata hoped to re-

establish an independent and priest-led Media.

H **Hellespont** (now Dardanelles).
Hydro-engineering projects undertaken by the Persians included the completion of a canal to link the Nile and Red Sea. They also repaired an Egyptian dam at Memphis.

I **Issus** (now Iskenderun in Turkey) was named Alexandretta in honour of Alexander the Great, conqueror of the Persians at Issus in 333 BC.

M **Magi,** the Median priests and scholars, later degenerated into tricksters. Their mysterious activities became known as

Gold armlet

Architecture, arts and language

The Achaemenians had several capitals: Susa was the main one, Pasargade another; Ecbatana was the summer capital and Babylon the winter capital. Each succeeding king tried to outdo his predecessors in architectural splendour. About 520 BC Darius I began the construction of a new capital — Parsai, known today by its Greek name, PERSEPOLIS and when it was completed some 150 years later it became one of the most impressive monuments of all time. This capital was also a shrine — the main centre for the New Year Festival (celebrated in spring). In art, the Persians borrowed freely from the peoples they had conquered.

Darius I and his court probably spoke Old Persian — an Indo-European language. Public business was quite likely conducted in Aramaic, because the Persians used local peoples for their civil servants. Perhaps it was these officials who developed from cuneiform, the 36 characters that formed the basic script of Persian writing. A few ideograms were sometimes used alongside the script. Avesta, the language of the Zoroastrian holy books was closely allied to Old Persian.

Agricultural life

The Achaemenian kings took a keen interest in forestry, agriculture and HYDRO-ENGINEERING. Once felled, trees were systematically replanted. Fruit trees from west of the Euphrates River were transplanted to the eastern empire and Persian pistachios were planted in Syria. The Persians planted rice in Mesopotamia and sesame in Egypt and experimented with viniculture. The land was worked by serfs and slaves employed on large estates. Main crops included wheat, barley and olives. The diet of rich and poor alike included meat, fish, bread, oil, wine and honey. Large estates provided for most of their own needs in clothing, furniture, and other everyday items. Under Persian government, living standards rose in most parts of the empire. The Persians kept the old waterways in good repair and constructed new ones.

Persian history

Cyrus early on faced a hostile coalition of Babylonia, Egypt, SPARTA and Lydia. With lightning speed he defeated and annexed Lydia before its allies could send aid. Then he prised Palestine

magic. The 'three wise men', stated in the Gospel of St Matthew to have visited the infant Jesus, were Magi.

Marathon, a plain 32 km north of Athens, was where the Athenians and their allies defeated the Persians in 490 BC, before the Spartans arrived.

Mithras appears as a sun god in the Indian sacred *Vedas* and as a warrior god in the Zoroastrian *Avesta*. Mithraism outlived Persia. Roman soldiers spread it throughout the Roman empire, including Britain.

Money. The first coins were minted by King CROESUS of Lydia, at Sardis in the 500s BC.

Mycale, a mountain in the coastal strip of Asia Minor, lay opposite Samos island. It is now called Mount Samsun. The Greeks defeated the Persian fleet there in 479 BC. This ended the struggle for European Greece and began the fight for Asia Minor.

P **Parthians** were probably a Scythian people. Parthia lay south-east of the Caspian Sea. The Parthian empire flourished about 100 BC to AD 226. It extended from the Euphrates to the Indus, and from the Oxus to the Indian Ocean. The Parthian civilization was not outstanding culturally.

Early Persian bull

Persepolis (*City of the Persians* in Greek), stood on a 12 metre high terrace extending 450 by 300 metres. On the terrace, palaces, monuments and offices were constructed. Main buildings included the *Apadana* (audience hall of Darius I) and the Hall of 100 columns.

Persia was that part of the empire north of the present-day Persian Gulf and Gulf of Oman, and south of ancient Media.

S **Sacae** (or Sakas), the nomadic Scythians of Persia's northern frontier, lived probably in the region of Chinese Sinkiang.

Salamis, an island west of Athens, was near where the

Sassanian king hunting

and part of Syria away from Babylonia and took Babylon itself in 539 BC. Cyrus annexed all Babylonia to the borders of Egypt. The PARTHIANS, BACTRIANS and SACAE also submitted to him.

Cyrus's son, CAMBYSES, speedily subdued and annexed Egypt in 525 BC. Several revolts then broke out against him and GAUMATA, a Magi from Media, usurped the throne. Cambyses died while hurrying back from Egypt, probably by suicide. A relative of his then killed Gaumata, crushed the rebellion, and installed himself as Darius I.

To protect the northern borders of his empire, Darius attacked the Scythian lands from east of the Caspian Sea to the Balkans west of the Black Sea. In the course of this attack, he annexed THRACE and Macedonia. Among the conquered Greeks of Asia Minor were the Ionians of the Aegean coastal strip. Ionia revolted in 499 BC, aided by Athens and this brought about a full-scale Persian attack on Greece. But the Greeks finally defeated the Persians at MARATHON in 490 BC.

XERXES I (who succeeded Darius I in 486 BC) assembled an army of 180,000 men. Using Phoenician vessels he built a double line of boats to bridge the HELLESPONT. In 480 BC his warriors advanced over it to defeat the Greeks at THERMOPYLAE. Xerxes pushed on to Athens, which he burned, but in the same year the Greeks defeated his fleet at SALAMIS. Fearful of being trapped without supplies, the main Persian force returned home. In 479 BC, the Greeks defeated the remnant of the Persian force.

Despite its victories, Greece remained weak because it was disunited, often at war within itself. The Persians kept control of Asia Minor and Cyprus by cleverly exploiting Greek divisions. However, Persia was in decline. It recovered quickly but briefly under ARTAXERXES III (reigned 358-337 BC), who retook Egypt, which had broken away.

A new power was rising in Greece. The Macedonians hammered most of Greece into a single state and invaded Asia Minor in 334 BC. In 333 BC, Alexander the Great of Macedon, defeated Darius III at the battle of ISSUS. Following further defeat in 331 BC, the Persian empire collapsed and disappeared as suddenly as it had begun.

Above: The surviving columns of Persepolis rise skyward behind the grand staircase sculptured to advertise the splendour and extent of the empire. Bringing tribute to Persia come Medes, Bactrians, Sogdians, Parthians, Elamites, Scythians, Assyrians, Thracians, Cilicians, Babylonians, Armenians, Indians, Afghans, Lydians, Cappadocians and Phoenicians. The double-headed bull capital (*below*) probably stood in front of the entrance hall of the 100-column palace.

allied Greek fleet defeated the Persian fleet in 480 BC.
Sardis, leading city of Asia Minor 650-546 BC, was the capital of Lydia.
Satrapies were originally 23 in number. In a clockwise direction from Fars (the Persian homeland) they were: Fars; Elam; Chaldea; Assyria; Arabaya (Mesopotamia, Syria, Phoenicia, Palestine combined); Egypt; Peoples of the Sea; Ionia; Lydia and Mysia; Media; Armenia; Cappadocia; Parthia and Hyrcania; Zarangia; Aria; Chorasmia; Bactria; Sogdiana; Gandhara; Sacae; Thata-

gus; Arachosia; Makas. Eight were added later.
Sparta, capital of the Greek state of Laconia (better known as Sparta), was cre-

Figure from Persepolis

ated by Dorian invaders. Sparta became the most warlike state in Greece. After 600 BC, Sparta was little more than an armed camp given wholly to war pursuits. Weakling boys were killed by exposure at birth.
Susa, the old Elamite capital, was destroyed by the Assyrians and rebuilt by the Persians.

T **Thermopylae,** a narrow pass in present-day central Greece (near Lamia), was the entrance into ancient Greece from the north. Its name means 'hot gates'

from the hot mineral springs near by.
Thrace was a perpetual battlefield and moved its boundaries often between 1300 BC and Roman times. Thrace was a Persian satrapy in the south-eastern-most corner of Europe (opposite the Sea of Marmara) about 512-479 BC.

X **Xerxes I** (c.519-465 BC) son of Darius the Great and grandson of Cyrus the Great, had several military successes. But his fleet lost the battle of SALAMIS. He was murdered in 465 BC by the

captain of his own bodyguard.

Z **Zoroaster** (Zarathustra in Persian) may have lived 660-583 BC or earlier. Possibly he was once a MAGI. He is the reputed founder of Zoroastrianism, but there is no certainty that he lived.
Zoroastrians. Zoroastrianism is still followed by the Parsees, descendants of Persians who moved to India and now number 150,000. Fire is sacred to the Parsees; earth and water should not be polluted.

The prophet Moses, David (who fought the giant Goliath), and the fabulous King Solomon — all are part of the Hebrew religious tradition that has spread its influence throughout the world and given us both Christianity and Islam.

The Hebrews

Right: The map shows the 'promised land' of the Jews, which from about 926 BC was divided into Israel in the north and Judea in the south. Distances were small; Jerusalem to Nazareth being only about 100 km, and Jerusalem to Mount Sinai about 450 km.

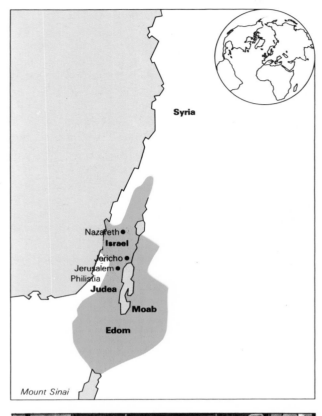

Syria

Nazareth●
Israel
Jericho●
Jerusalem●
Philistia
Judea
Moab
Edom
Mount Sinai

Right: The *Torah,* read by being unwound from rollers as required, contains the 5 books of the law traditionally given to Moses by God on Mount Sinai. The *Torah* is read by Christians as the first part of the Old Testament.

Most of our knowledge of the HEBREWS (or JEWS) before Roman times comes from the Jewish Bible, known by Christians as the Old Testament. But the Hebrews also appear in Egyptian records about 1200 BC. They fled from captivity in Egypt to settle in the less fertile parts of Canaan. They were then developing the worship of one supreme, invisible God (Yahweh) and despised their neighbours for worshipping idols.

The Jews were weak militarily and had little political influence. Their land was usually dominated by great powers such as Egypt, Assyria and Babylon. But their religion of Judaism, backed by its dynamic literature, became highly influential. From it stemmed two even more powerful religions, Christianity and Islam.

The covenant with God

The Hebrews did not easily accept the idea of one invisible God. When their leader, MOSES, went up to Mount Sinai to receive the TEN COMMANDMENTS from God, the people rebelled. They demanded that AARON (Moses's brother) should make them gods such as other tribes had. Yielding, he moulded them a golden calf to worship. But later the Hebrews entered into a COVENANT with Yahweh. By this they became his 'CHOSEN PEOPLE' whom he would protect and help. In return, the Hebrews promised not to follow other gods and to accept God's law.

Once in Canaan, the Hebrews were at first led by JUDGES — men and women picked for their wisdom. But the authority of the judges often depended upon whether they had the support of PROPHETS (men believed to communicate the will of God). The Hebrews called their high priests and kings messiahs. Later, the prophets foretold that an ideal king would come to lead Israel. They said he would be a direct descendant of DAVID, a Hebrew hero-king. This future ideal

Reference

A Aaron was the brother of Moses and Miriam. Aaron represented the priesthood.
Abraham, according to the Bible, was the traditional father of the JEWS. At 75 years of age he was told by God to move to Canaan. God is also said to have promised Abraham that his descendants would inherit Canaan.
Ahaz, king of JUDEA (reigned c.735-715 BC), refused to join Israel and Syria in war against Assyria. When the 2 countries invaded Judea, Ahaz gave Assyria aid to defeat them. But he then became Assyria's vassal. Ahaz's policies were opposed by the prophet Isaiah.
Ammonites, 'sons of Ammon', were said to be descended from Lot, Abraham's nephew.
Antiochus Epiphanes seized the throne of Syria with Rome's approval. He was also ruler of Judea from about 175-164 BC. He tried to replace Judaism by the Greek religion, but failed. Judea revolted and broke

away from Rome.

C Chosen people were the Israelites (or Jews). In Judaist belief, Yahweh, or God, chose to make his covenant with them.
Covenant was a common device with nomadic peoples, among whom written documents were rare. It was a verbal agreement or bargain made in ritual circumstances, and had the force of law. A curse was believed to fall on those who broke it. Yahweh made a covenant with the Israelites that they would worship him alone.

D David was a youthful hero who slew the Philistine giant Goliath. He

Sacrifice of Aaron

fought for both Israel and Philistia. Eventually, he succeeded SAUL as king of Israel.

E Edomites lived in Edom between the Dead Sea and the Gulf of Aqaba about 1200-700 BC. They were said to be descended from Esau, brother of Jacob.
Ezra, an expert on the law of Moses went from Babylon to Judea about 458 BC or earlier. He forced men who had married foreign wives to leave them and the children.

H Hebrews is the earliest term for the Israelites,

king became known as the MESSIAH.

The Hebrew Bible was probably written between 1200 and 150 BC. It is one of the greatest literary works of all time and stories from it are known throughout the world. It is not one book, but a collection of books. The first five books, the *Torah* (Law), laid down the pattern of life to be followed by the Hebrews. After AD 200 another set of writings, the *Talmud,* was compiled as a guide to the laws and religious teachings. The Bible was almost entirely in Hebrew, which used a script derived from Aramaic. Spoken Hebrew had almost died out by 100 BC, after which most Jews probably spoke Aramaic, retaining Hebrew as the language of prayer.

History of the Israelites

Traditionally, the *patriarchs* (fathers) of the Hebrews were ABRAHAM, his son ISAAC, and grandson Jacob (renamed ISRAEL). They may have lived about 1900 BC. Abraham migrated from Mesopotamia into Canaan (Palestine). Later, the Israelites (descendants of Israel) settled in Egypt. About 1300 BC they were reduced in status to slaves. According to the Bible, Moses led them out of Egypt in search of the 'promised land' of Canaan, and they journeyed 40 years through the desert.

Moses's successor, JOSHUA, led the Hebrews into Canaan probably about 1200 BC. They were forced to settle in the hills because enemies, notably the Philistines, occupied the more fertile coastal plain. Other tribes also warred with the Israelites, including the EDOMITES, MOABITES and AMMONITES.

The TWELVE TRIBES of Israel were ruled

Left: The tents of the Israelites, referred to in the early books of the Bible, probably resembled those of present-day Bedouin.

Above: The Dead Sea Scrolls, discovered in 1947, are the oldest-known manuscripts of the Bible. They include parts of all the books of the Hebrew Bible except Esther. The scrolls probably formed part of a library of the Essenes, a Jewish sect flourishing about 100 BC to AD 70. A Bedouin boy found them preserved in a cave.

separately by judges. About 1020 BC they united and chose SAUL for their king, against the advice of the prophet Samuel. Saul was followed by David and his son SOLOMON. About 926 BC the tribes quarrelled. Ten tribes broke away to form the kingdom of Israel in the north, while the other two tribes (Benjamin and Judah) set up the kingdom of JUDEA in the south. War followed between them, but stronger powers decided their destinies.

Both Israel and Judea became tributary states of Assyria, and King AHAZ of Judea gained Assyrian aid from TIGLATH-PILESER III against invasion, by Israel and Syria. In 721 BC, the Assyrians finally destroyed Israel and dispersed its people.

The kingdom of Judea

After Babylonia had destroyed Assyria, it annexed Judea in 587 BC. Although Judea survived, its leading citizens were taken as captives to Babylon. After Cyrus the Persian conquered Babylon in 539 BC, he allowed the Judean community to return home. For a time, Judea came under the control of EZRA (a priest), and of NEHEMIAH, who acted as Persian governor. When Persia collapsed, Alexander the Great took Judea in 334 BC. He and his successors allowed the Judeans to practise their religion unhindered. When King ANTIOCHUS EPIPHANES tried to reverse this policy in 168 BC, the Judeans successfully rebelled. United under JUDAS MACCABAEUS they managed to defeat their Syrian

---

and also the Judeans.

Isaac, son of ABRAHAM and father of Jacob (ISRAEL).
Israel (Jacob) was the father of 10 sons from whom descended the TWELVE TRIBES of Israel.

Jesus of Nazareth was probably born in 4 BC or earlier. He was a Jew and a revolutionary thinker whose followers believed him to be the Son of God (the Christ). The Jewish priestly authorities feared that Jesus' teachings and their political consequences threatened

their position. In about AD 29 he was tortured and then crucified.
Jews originally meant Judahites (members of the tribe of Judah). It has now generally replaced the earlier term HEBREWS.
Joshua, the assistant and successor of Moses, conquered part of Canaan. Traditionally, the walls of Jericho fell down at the blast of the Israelite trumpets.
Judas Maccabaeus led the resistance to ANTIOCHUS EPIPHANES and freed Judea from Syrian domination about 168 BC.

Judea, the southern Hebrew state, existed 926 BC-70 AD. It was composed of the tribes of Benjamin and Judah, and its capital was Jerusalem.
Judges led the Israelites after they settled in Canaan and before SAUL became king. Important judges included Deborah (a prophetess); Gideon (a warrior); Samson (a giant whose strength lasted only while his hair was long) and Samuel (the first PROPHET).

M Messiah in Hebrew means 'anointed one'.

Christos or *Christ* has the same meaning in Greek. The Jews waited for the Messiah (ideal king) to lead Israel. Their priests rejected JESUS

David

as the Messiah, and he was crucified by the Romans.
Moabites lived in Moab, east of the Dead Sea. They fortified their towns against the Israelites and refused them passage through Moabite territory. Moab plundered Judea after its defeat by Babylonia.
Moses, according to tradition, was found floating in a basket in the bullrushes by Pharaoh's daughter, who adopted him. (His story parallels that of Sargon of Akkad.) In the Bible, Moses had a vision and saw Yahweh in a burning bush.

overlord and won independence for nearly 100 years.

In 63 BC, the Romans took the Judean capital of Jerusalem. About 97 years later, JESUS OF NAZARETH was arrested. Some Jews thought he was the MESSIAH or 'anointed one', but the Jewish priestly leaders rejected this and urged PILATE (the Roman officer governing Judea) to have him crucified. The Judeans tried a revolt against Rome in AD 66, but in AD 70 the Romans crushed them. There was a further uprising the following century, from AD 132–135. This also failed and, during the next few hundred years, most Jews then left Judea, which disappeared from the map.

Below: Houses of poor Hebrews in Israel and Judea were single-roomed, box-like structures made of clay. Inside, the dark room lit only by small high windows, contrasted with the blazing sunlight outside. The family slept on a raised section of the floor, or on the flat roof which served as a second room, and was reached by an outside staircase. Each house had its own courtyard, within which goats and donkeys might be kept by families that could afford them. The illustration shows that dress in Biblical times differed little from the clothing still worn by many people in the Middle East. Oil lamps gave light and water had to be carried laboriously from wells, springs or rivers. The right to use a particular source of water was often disputed. While men worked outside the house, women washed and cooked in the courtyard. Roofs stood about 3.5 metres above floor level, supported by wooden beams over which brushwood, clay and straw was laid.

Yahweh told him to lead the children of Israel out of bondage in Egypt, but the Israelites rebelled against him several times. After leaving Egypt the Israelites had to spend 40 years in the desert. Few who set out reached the 'promised land'.

Nehemiah was the butler of King Artaxerxes of Persia, and when he took an interest in the unhappy plight of Judea about 445 BC, the king made him its governor and allowed him to rebuild its walls. His policies resembled those of EZRA.

Pilate, the Roman officer governing Judea, sentenced Jesus to crucifixion. He did so at the request of Caiaphas and other

Elijah and the ravens

priests who claimed Jesus was a blasphemer because of his Messianic claims. The Romans saw in him a danger to their rule.
Prophets were those believed to be called by God to speak for him. They were thought to have the powers of *seers* (those who can foretell events). Consequently, they held influence over judges and kings. Leading prophets included Elijah (about 850 BC), Elisha, Isaiah, Jeremiah and Ezekiel. The prophets stressed the ideals of social justice and morality.

Saul, first king of Israel, had to fight against the iron spears of the Philistines. Defeated and wounded, he died by falling on his sword.
Solomon, son of DAVID, became Israel's third king, but his extravagant and un-Jewish way of life led to revolts. After his death, the Kingdom divided.

Ten commandments were that the Hebrews should: have no other gods but the one God; not make idols; not take God's name in vain; keep the sabbath day holy; honour their pa-

rents; not kill; not commit adultery; not steal; not lie; not covet anything belonging to others.
Twelve tribes of Israel were: Reuben, Simeon, Judah, Dan, Naphtali, Gad, Asher, Issachar, Zebulun, Benjamin (Jacob's sons), Ephraim and Manasseh (Jacob's grandsons).

The ancient Chinese were a great nation of traders who exported silk and spices, bronze and jade to the far corners of the known world. With their iron tools they built the Great Wall of China, the only man-made edifice to be seen from the moon.

The Early Chinese

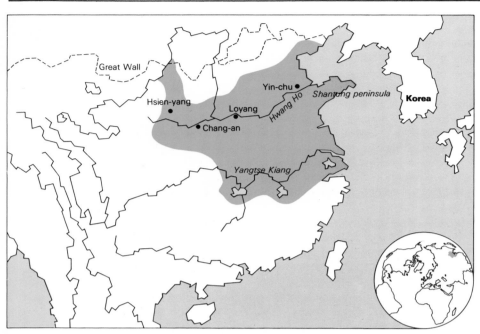

It was between the time of Hammurabi of Babylon and the fall of Crete that Chinese civilization began to emerge about 1600 BC. Its centre was due east of Persia beyond the mountain barriers of Central Asia in the valley of the HWANG HO (Yellow River) where settlers cultivated the fertile soil and kept cattle and sheep. From the 1500s to about 1028 BC this settlement was ruled by the SHANG DYNASTY. This was followed by the CHOU DYNASTY (1027–221 BC); the CHIN DYNASTY (221–206 BC); and the HAN DYNASTY (206 BC to AD 220).

Floods and barbarians: the twin dangers

The life-giving Hwang Ho was the Chinese people's source of food, but in times of flood the river became their most dangerous enemy and flood control was one of the two basic tasks of every emperor. The other great task was to protect the northern frontier of the civilization

Above: Han China expanded to encompass an empire bigger than that of any other dynasty for the next 1500 years.

Above: This bronze wine vessel shaped like an owl was used in ceremonies 3,000 years ago.

against invasion by nomadic Mongol tribes. Under the Chou dynasty the country was split into several vassal kingdoms, each of which built a defensive wall against the BARBARIANS. When the state of Chin hammered the other kingdoms into one unified country, it linked all the walls into the GREAT WALL OF CHINA. Inside this wall, the Chinese, sometimes united, sometimes divided, developed a single culture that has existed for an unbroken period of over 3,500 years.

Early Chinese society

China's first important dynasty, the Shang, had a feudal structure with the court and nobles ruling over peasants and slaves. In the country the slaves worked the land, while in large towns such as YIN-CHU (Anyang), the last Shang capital, they were employed in workshops.

Shang dynasty cities and villages were walled and their buildings were of wood, with large rectangular halls raised on earthen platforms. By 1,000 BC, the total Shang population probably exceeded four millions, occupying an area about the size of modern Spain or the ancient Assyrian empire. The Shang rulers needed more labour and carried out slave-raiding expeditions on the fringes of their empire. A nomadic people, called the Chou, eventually retaliated. They fought with deadly crossbows and new, efficient CHARIOTS and finally caused the downfall of the Shang. The vassal kings of the Chou then took over most of the Hwang Ho and Yangtse Kiang basins.

Working the land

Chou rulers set up a string of village communes known as the CHING TIEN SYSTEM, whereby each family in the commune was allotted a piece of land, but was bound to co-operate with the others in farming the whole area as efficiently as possible. Each Chou commune was largely self-

Reference

B **Barbarians,** to the Chinese, were any peoples not inside their own borders. To the Shang, the Chou were barbarians.
Bone was a useful material in ancient China. Some of the earliest surviving pictographs are found on human skulls and are known as oracle bone characters.

C **Calendar.** In Shang China the year was divided into 12 months of 29 or 30 days (reckoned to be the full cycle of the moon). An extra month was added every few years.
Ceramics were made in China from prehistoric times. The scarcity of metals probably encouraged the Chinese to concentrate on developing their techniques with pottery. Partial glazing was used from the 200s BC. Han ceramics may have been influenced by ideas which came from Rome via the silk route.
Chang-an was the capital of the Western Han (202 BC to AD 25) and some later dynas-

ties. Chang Chiao, founder of a religious cult, led the YELLOW TURBANS in revolt against the Eastern Han in AD 184.

Chariots came into use with horse-breeding and riding. Shang 2-wheeled chariots carried 3 men and may have been a version of the Hittite chariot taken into China by Mongol Turks.
Chin dynasty was officially founded in 221 BC, but the Chou emperor abdicated power to the king of Chin in 256 BC. The Chin united the country and named it China.
Ching tien system was so called because land was divided into plots shaped like the character 'ching'. From time to time, land allotted to families was reallocated to

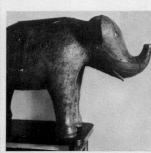

Sacrificial vessel: early Chou

ensure that everyone had a share of good land and bad.
Chou dynasty was divided into Western Chou (c.1028-771 BC) and Eastern Chou (770-221 BC). Unable to hold back the Mongol tribes, Emperor Ping abandoned his western territories in 771 BC. He set up the Eastern Chou capital at Loyang in 770 BC. The Chou emperors gradually lost power to vassal kings.
Coins, or coin-like objects, circulated widely in China before 400 BC. They were bronze replicas of spades, billhooks, knives and other tools. Cowrie shells passed

sufficient, and quite highly developed.

The land was tilled with animal-drawn ploughs and manure was worked into the ground. Every so often the fields were left fallow to 'rest' them. Two-pronged wooden hoes were used to plant rice, wheat and millet, and crops were harvested with sickles of stone and shell. BONE was also used to make weapons, tools and writing materials. Animal farming included cattle, pigs, sheep, dogs and chickens, and wild animals were also hunted for their meat, sometimes from horseback. To the Chou, horses were a prized possession and used for pulling royal carts and war chariots.

Silk was produced in southern China from prehistoric times and the silk industry prospered particularly under the Shang and Chou dynasties who used advanced weaving techniques. Silk was worn by the rich; the less well-off wore clothing of skins, furs, flax or leather.

Iron and trade

Iron ploughs and tools came into general use by 700 BC. These, and advanced techniques, improved the productivity of farming and increased its scale. As capital and expenditure grew, the ching tien system died out. Land came under the control of nobles and rich peasants and disputes between states became so frequent that 475–221 BC is called the WARRING STATES PERIOD.

The demand for iron in agriculture brought a mining boom. Smelting works and metal working factories employed hundreds of workers making, amongst other things, spades. These iron spades had a direct influence on the expansion of trade, for they enabled more canals to be dug. The rising state of Chin cut a 150-kilometre canal which transformed 250,000 hectares of wasteland into farmland, besides forming an important trade route. Another waterway linked the Yangtse Kiang and other rivers into an integrated transport system, along which many new cities developed. By 400 BC, perhaps 25 million Chou people occupied an area twice as large as the old Shang territory.

Prosperity reached a high peak under Emperor WU of the Han dynasty (reigned 141-86 BC). While fighting the HSIUNG NU (Mongol Huns) he discovered that a secret and profitable trade was being carried along the 'silk route' between China and south-western Asia. Realizing its potential, he brought the trade under government control, providing protection for the caravans against the Hsiung Nu and other robbers. Chinese bronzes, jades, lacquer-wares, CERAMICS and, above all, silks travelled westwards to Damascus, Rome, Spain and even distant Britain. Eastwards into China went rugs and carpets, frankincense, camphor, coral, plants, birds, HORSES and other animals.

Above: Human skull bones provided a writing material for some of the earliest-known Chinese characters.

Above: Early Chinese characters showed things in 'matchstick' form (*top*). These later developed into present-day characters (*bottom*). Both forms are shown for a tree (*left*) and a goat (*right*).

Left: Rice has been an important crop of China since earliest known times, especially in the south. It was not, however, the main food until after Han times. In Chou China people ate much beef and mutton; in Chin and Han times people ate reduced quantities of meat and switched to pork and dog meat because pigs and dogs required less land. Wheat was then the main crop, but rice replaced it in southern China in AD 300–600. In northern China, the rich ate rice; the poor, wheat.

as small change. Round coins with a hole in the centre (called cash) came into use about 250 BC and are still used today. The first Chin emperor superseded all coins by new round ones with a hole.
Confucius (c.551-c.479 BC) is the Latinized name of Kung Fu-tzu. He was a philosopher concerned above all with morality and right behaviour which were embodied in tradition.

G Great Wall of China was built by a Chin emperor who conscripted

some 30% of the male population of China to link earlier walls into a 2,400 km-long towered frontier barrier. The importance of the wall lay in

Chü-Yang Gate: Great Wall

the watchmen who patrolled it and who lit beacon fires to alert mobile troops against approaching invaders. It is the only man-made object that can be seen from the moon.

H Han dynasty was founded by LIU PANG in 206 BC. After the civil war, the Han capital of Chang-an was captured by the HSIUNG NU. LIU HSIN then set up the Eastern Han dynasty (AD 25-220) with its capital at the old Eastern Chou capital, Loyang.
Horses were rare and valu-

able in China. The Han emperor Wu sent 100,000 soldiers into Ferghana (near the old Persian empire's border) to seize horses refused him by Ferghana's king. Wu got his horses, but 40,000 soldiers perished from thirst, hunger, disease or exposure in the bleak lands of central Asia.
Hsia dynasty (2000s to 1500s BC) is known only in legend. Its supposed earliest chief was Huang Ti (Yellow Emperor), and its earliest legend concerns flood control on the Yellow River.
Hsiung Nu were nomadic

tribes pushed northward by the first Chin emperor. Having lost their best pasture land to China, they founded the tribal federation

Model horses: Han

The Emperor Wu benefited personally from the prosperity of his people. He laid out the Imperial park of the Han emperors in Chang-an, vast ornamental gardens bounded by a wall over 160 kilometres long, where Indian rhinoceroses roamed with other exotic animals in a setting of groves, lakes and springs.

Religion and philosophy

The twin religions of China are TAOISM and Confucianism, the teachings of CONFUCIUS. Both originated in the 500s BC and can be considered as PHILOSOPHIES rather than religions. They have also played an important part in forming the Chinese character.

Above: The Great Wall of China, built as a defence against the Mongols, absorbed the forced labour of 30% of China's manpower in Chin dynasty times, over 2,200 years ago. When built it linked existing stretches of fortified boundaries into a continuous one that extended 3,200 km. In recent centuries it has been extensively restored.

known as the Hsiung Nu. Their first chief was Touman and during Han times they may have numbered over 2 million. They attacked China's border for 500 years.

Hwang Ho. A river that rises in Tibet and flows mainly eastwards across northern China. Following a flood in AD 1852, its course shifted 400 km to the north so that it entered the sea north, instead of south, of the Shantung peninsula. It was long known to the Chinese as 'China's sorrow' or 'Scourge of the Sons of Han' because of its severe flooding. The name Hwang Ho (Yellow River) comes from the *loess* (yellow earth) which is carried along in its waters.

J Jade was from ancient times used in religious ceremonies and made into jewellery. Carved into the shape of a man and worn as an amulet, it was believed to ward off disease and evil spirits. The bodies of a Han prince and his wife, clothed in pieces of jade sewn together with gold thread, were excavated in AD 1968.

L Language of China has no alphabet and each Chinese character conveys one complete idea. The early Chinese characters were pictures, but in time, characters became more abstract. Learning to read and write in Chinese is more difficult than in alphabetical languages, and nowadays about 3,000 characters must be learned to be able to read a newspaper, but the communication of ideas is quicker.

Liu Hsiu reigned AD 25-57 as Kuang-wu, first emperor of the Eastern Han dynasty.

Liu Pang, a minor official from a peasant family, was one of many leaders who

Jade funeral suit of Princess Ton Wan

Bronze leopard: Han

Confucianism teaches loyalty to the family, ancestor worship, and obedience to the laws of society. It puts the accent on ceremonies, order, and the 'proper' ways of doing things. Taoism, summed up in the *Tao Te Ching* ('The Way and its Power'), ridicules Confucianist ceremonies and rules of behaviour. It says that men should always work in harmony with nature, never against it. Taoism incorporates many deities which have been worshipped from earliest times and are organized like the earthly royal court. Below the Jade emperor, the chief god, were the Moon goddess, the Rain, Wind and Thunder gods, the gods of Wealth, Happiness, Walls and Ditches, the Kitchen, and so on. The god of Examinations was probably inspired by the Confucians, who imposed on China a strict examination system for those who wanted to become MANDARINS (senior civil servants).

Arts, language and science

Developments in arts and language in ancient China were related to the demands of religion and trade. Bronze urns, often in animal shapes, were used for making sacrifices, preparing food and exporting, as were lacquerware, ceramics and JADE, which was regarded as a product of heaven. Chinese pictographic LANGUAGE was developed to record early works of literature, poetry set to music, the works of Confucianist tradition and rival philosophies, and mythology. Contact with the 'barbarians' introduced war songs, dances and MONGOL DRAMA into China.

Consistent with the Chinese character, science was regarded as of little value unless it could be directly related to practical purposes, such as hydro-engineering, agriculture, metallurgy, the CALENDAR, and weights and measures, which were especially important in trade and taxation. The early Chinese also studied mathematics, astronomy and engineering and exchanged philosophical and scientific ideas with Persia.

History

The Shang dynasty was established in the 1500s BC when a tribal chief named Tang overthrew

Above: The wrestlers, a bronze of late Chou times, shows 2 identical men poised in opposite directions with their hands joined.

Below: Confucius, the great Chinese teacher of 2,500 years ago, is seen surrounded by his pupils in this silk painting.

Above: A bronze flying horse of the Eastern Han dynasty symbolizes the horses imported from Ferghana and Sogdiana. The 'gallop' was shown more accurately than in any European paintings before AD 1700.

Above right: This pottery model of a Han house was entombed with a dead man to provide him with a house in the next world.

Chieh, the last ruler of the legendary Hsia dynasty. About 1028 BC, King Wu of the Chou defeated the last Shang emperor at Muyeh, near his capital, and set up the Western Chou dynasty. Many small vassal kingdoms came into being, owing allegiance to the Chou emperors. In 771 BC, the Western Chou were overwhelmed by the Yen Yun and Jung tribes. The defeated Chou emperor, Ping, moved his capital eastwards to LOYANG and began the Eastern Han empire in 770 BC. Five hundred years of border and internal wars followed and in 256 BC the last Chou emperor abdicated power to the king of Chin.

Chin systematically crushed each neighbour, Han, Wei, Chu, Chi, Chao and Yen, and annexed them. In 221 BC (when Rome was preparing for its second war against Carthage), the king of Chin took the title of Shi Huang Ti (First Emperor). In his new role he pressed millions of unwilling peasants into forced labour for ambitious building projects.

During the reign of the Second Emperor, 900 army conscripts found themselves unable to reach their frontier position on time because of

floods. To arrive late would mean certain death, so they killed their commander and became outlaws. Their revolt sparked off a revolution and soon, the Chin capital of Hsien-yang fell to the peasant armies, led by LIU PANG. After defeating his rivals in 202 BC, Liu Pang became Eminent Emperor, first ruler of the Han dynasty. Once established, he managed to buy off a threatened attack by 300,000 Hsiung Nu horsemen. But under the rule of Wu, they returned again to attack the Han capital, CHANG-AN, and Wu drove them back in three bloody wars (127, 122, and 119 BC).

Wang Mang, a regent, usurped the throne in AD 8 and introduced reforms. Civil war followed, and in AD 25, LIU HSIU (a deposed Han prince) set up the Eastern Han dynasty at Loyang. Western Han territory (including the silk route) was lost to the Hsiung Nu. In AD 184, Chang Chiao led the rebellion of a million yellow-turbanned peasants. The imperial army crushed the YELLOW TURBANS, and swept away the last Han ruler. As a result of this revolt the Han empire disintegrated in 220 AD.

never existed. Legend has it that he once met CONFUCIUS and advised him to discard all his ideas, and many people believe that he wrote the *Tao Te Ching,* the chief book of Taoism. Taoism deplores human striving and encourages submission to nature. It has never sought converts.

W Warring States period (475-221 BC) was in the later half of Eastern Chou times. As the dynasty weakened, 7 kingdoms (Chi, Chu, Yen, Chin, Han, Chao and Wei) grew stronger and

warred with one another, mainly for territory. Eventually, Chin won.
Wu, emperor of Western Han, reigned for 55 years. He

Taoist mountain symbol

was the hammer of the HSIUNG NU and also conquered western Turkestan, western Korea and southern China. Wu promoted trade with the west and sent emmissaries to the Romans. Han China prospered under him, but social and economic problems remained unsolved and in time destroyed the dynasty.

Y Yellow Turbans were a rebel peasant army so known because of the headdresses they wore when they rose against the Eastern Han dynasty in 184 BC. The

official Han priests and the ceremonies and sacrifices they laid down were unpopular with the peasants and uprisings were common. A previous revolt against Wang Mang had been fought by the Red Eyebrows, a peasant army who had no uniforms and so dyed their eyebrows as a mark of recognition. The leader of the Yellow Turbans was Chang Chiao, founder of a religious cult known as 'Taiping Tao', who won their confidence by curing diseases.
Yin-chu, the sixth and final

Shang capital, stood on the site of Anyang. The Shang capital had to be changed 5 times because of the flooding of the Hwang Ho.

Han painting

The rigid social structure imposed on the Indian sub-continent by the Aryans still exists today. Social and political life was greatly influenced by the three religions, Hinduism, Jainism and Buddhism.

The Early Indians

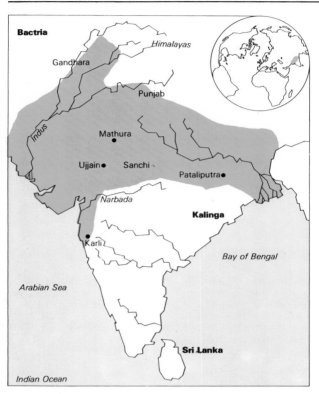

Above: The map shows Maurya India at the height of its influence under the Buddhist King Asoka, about 250 BC.

Left: This finely carved sandstone figure from Lahore presents the Buddha in the pose of a Yogi ascetic: the soles of his feet up, his hands positioned for turning the Wheel of the Law.

The triangular subcontinent of India is hemmed in by the snow-capped Himalayas to the north, and by other mountains to the north-east. These mountains and the surrounding seas form a natural 'Great Wall of India' and only the north-west, the area which is now Pakistan, is accessible by land. Through this north-western frontier came many invaders. The most important were the Aryans who fought their way into India about 1500 BC, shortly after Shang China began. It took the Aryans about 1200 years to conquer most of the subcontinent, but at its height under King ASOKA the Aryan empire equalled that of Chin China in area. This unified area of India broke up, however, just at the moment when China achieved unity under the Chin.

Caste and religion in early India

The Aryans imposed a rigid social order based on CASTE. From birth, people were classified as either *Brahmins* (priests and scholars); *Kshatriyas* (rulers and warriors): *Vaisyas* (merchants, craftsmen and peasants); or *Sudras* (unskilled labourers). There were hundreds of sub-castes based on hereditary occupations, while at the very bottom were OUTCASTES. The Aryans brought a vast number of DEITIES into India and in time, Aryan and DRAVIDIAN gods fused to form an interrelated hierarchy of one religion — HINDUISM.

The only way out of the CASTE SYSTEM was to adopt JAINISM or BUDDHISM — two alternative religions. Jains held all life sacred and revered 24 saints or *Jainas*. Buddhism was founded by Siddhartha Gautama, a north Indian kshatriya, later known as Buddha. He taught the way to 'Enlightenment' which can be reached only when a man secures release from perpetual rebirth. Buddha taught that the way to end rebirth and suffering is to end the selfish desire that causes it. This was a difficult concept for people to

Reference

A **Aryan languages** of northern India that are now official languages include Hindi, Punjabi, Kashmiri, Gujarati, Marathi, Bengali, Assamese and Oriya. The scripts of all these languages derive from *Brahmi* – the script in which Asoka's laws were written.
Asoka, the warrior king who turned Buddhist, was the grandson of CHANDRAGUPTA. A 4 lion capital from an Asokan pillar is the emblem of modern India. Such pillars had writing carved on them stating Asoka's Buddhist beliefs and principles of government.

B **Bindusara,** son of CHANDRAGUPTA, extended the Maurya empire south into Dravidian India.
Buddhism is both a philosophy and a religion. Buddhists believe that the universe functions according to principles that cannot be altered by men or gods. Buddha (born Siddhartha Gautama) advised men to end suffering, which all endured, by following the *Noble Eightfold Path* of right views, right aims or motive, right speech, right acts, right livelihood, right effort, right concentration, and right contemplation. Buddha also advised following the *Middle Way,* avoiding extremes of hardship or luxury. After his death in c.483 BC, devotees made him a god and saints and other deities were soon worshipped alongside him. Buddhism spread and Asoka's son and daughter took it into Sri Lanka. Buddhism flourished in China from AD 400, and later in Korea, Tibet, Japan, Mongolia and south-eastern Asia.

Starving Buddha, Lahore

C **Caste system** in India was 2-fold. Brahmins, Kshatriyas, Vaisyas and Sudras can be thought of as hereditary classes. About 1000 BC, other caste divisions emerged, based on occupa-

A follower of Vishnu

Left: The *Jataka Tales*, legends of Buddha's former lives on earth, are illustrated in this carving on a stone pillar at Sanchi, India. Ordinary people, unlearned in Buddhist holy books, took their ideas of Buddhist principles from these fascinating stories.

understand and as a result Buddhism soon gathered its own collection of popular deities.

The main dynasty in early India was the Maurya. Maurya India was a land of villages closely supervised by the central government at Pataliputra, the capital. The Maurya emperors stockpiled food against possible famine, and built new villages so as to distribute the population more evenly. Although rice was the main crop and diet, MEAT was more commonly eaten in Maurya India than in later times.

Government activities

The government kept harbours, sanitation and water supply in good repair and engineers built roads and canals and kept them well maintained. Censuses were conducted and records of business transactions kept. People were compelled to take precautions against fire, and were fined for littering the city streets. Mining, tree felling and other activities connected with land were strictly controlled. Gambling was permitted, and taxed at five per cent, but the government's main income came from taxing farmers. The Mauryas also kept a large standing army.

The brain behind the government of CHANDRA-

Below: Krishna, dark-skinned and most popular of Indian deities, was a fun-loving god, yet finally perished as a warrior in war.

Below: Lakshmi, golden-skinned wife of Vishnu, emerged from a milk ocean. She is revered especially by merchants as the goddess of fortune.

Below: The 4-armed god Vishnu is the preserver of the universe. His 10 incarnations are said to include Krishna and Buddha.

Below: Varaha, the boar and third incarnation of Vishnu. After killing a demon, Varaha raised the earth on his tusk out of the universal ocean.

Below: Brahma, once supreme god of the Hindus, has long been replaced by the more popular gods, Siva and Vishnu. His 4 heads denote wisdom.

tions. The caste system still functions in India, but discrimination on caste grounds is illegal.
Cave temples were cut from solid rock by Buddhists, Jains and Hindus. One of the most impressive is at Karli (near Bombay). Buddhists cut this temple 38 metres into the rock during the first century AD.
Chandragupta, supposedly once a prisoner of Alexander the Great, founded the Maurya empire (324-313 BC).

D **Deities** of Hinduism supposedly number 330

A Jain temple, Mount Abu

million and differ from village to village. Today about 100 deities are of prime importance, the key ones being Siva (the creator and destroyer) and Vishnu (the preserver). Old gods, such as Indra and Brahma, are now seldom worshipped.
Dravidian languages of southern India (now official) are Tamil, Telegu, Kannada (Canarese) and Malayalam.
Dravidian sailors crossed the Indian Ocean to Burma and Malaya. Their routes were part of a larger trading system linking the Mediterranean to the East Indies. Possibly the Indians set sail to search for gold and silver after nomadic tribes cut the supply routes through central Asia in the 200s BC. The

Indians planted their Hindu–Buddhist culture in Thailand, Cambodia and Indonesia, especially Bali.
Dravidians were the pre-Aryan, darker-skinned people of India who were pushed southwards.

G **Gandhara,** a region in north-western India, came under Persian control before falling to Alexander the Great. It became part of Maurya India, then fell to Indo-Greeks, Sakas and Parthians. By AD 100 it had become the centre of a Buddhist-Greek style of

sculpture and architecture. Muslims swept away its art style about AD 700.

Gandharan sculptured head

GUPTA (first Maurya emperor) was KAUTILYA. This minister wrote the *Arthasastra* ('Manual of Politics') advising kings how to hold on to power. No one should oppress the people except the king himself, ruled Kautilya. This principle was applied in the law courts and yet Chandragupta ruled as a despot, setting spies on his officials and executing or maiming those who opposed him. Kautilya confessed that he knew no way of controlling corruption among officials.

Arts and languages

Chandragupta's palace is said to have rivalled those of the Persian kings in splendour. But, because it was built of wood (like almost all early Indian buildings), nothing survives of it. When the Buddhists came to build STUPAS, their stone gateways and balustrades were shaped in the fashion of earlier wooden buildings.

While Hindu sculpture was full of lively movement, Buddhist sculpture was serene. At first, Buddha was portrayed only by symbols, such as alms bowls. Later, superb Buddhas were carved and CAVE TEMPLES were cut out of solid rock. Art usually followed either the GANDHARA or MATHURA styles. Hindu, Jain and Buddhist

LITERATURE was vast in volume. The Hindu epic RAMAYANA is the fount of much Hindu legend and culture. India's ARYAN LANGUAGES derived from Sanskrit. In the south, DRAVIDIAN LANGUAGES were spoken.

DRAVIDIAN SAILORS from southern India braved the Indian Ocean to trade with south-

Above: The huge Buddhist stupa constructed at Sanchi in western India soon after the death of the Buddha, contains relics of him. It almost certainly comprises the oldest surviving Indian buildings. The stone balustrade resembles earlier wooden ones.

Below: Siva, god of both destruction and creation, ensures the regeneration of all things. He is often shown as Lord of the Dance in a ring of fire.

Below: Parvati, wife of Siva and mother of Ganesha, is known as 'the mountaineer', being the daughter of a Himalayan god.

Below: Ganesha, round-bellied with 4 arms and an elephant's head, is the god of wisdom, revered as the remover of obstacles.

Below: Manasa, a serpent goddess, is worshipped especially in Bengal. Snakes often appeared in Hindu myths, probably because they were feared.

Below: Hanuman, the monkey god (or sometimes merely the monkey king) was one of the heroes of the epic *Ramayana*.

Hinduism is older than history and has no known founder. The central theme in Hinduism is the belief in a Supreme Spirit, *Brahman*. Hindus worship vast numbers of deities and many animals and plants are sacred to them. The *Vedas* (Hindu sacred writings) carry more authority than the deities.

J Jainism is claimed to be immensely old. But in its present form it dates from the 500s BC when Mahavira formulated it. Jains believe Mahavira to be the latest of

24 tirthankaras (Jainas, or saints). According to mythology Rishabha, first tirthankara, lived for 8,400,000 years and stood 500 bows high.

Jain follower

Earthly beings are believed to be reborn a million times; deities, 400,000 times. There is clearly a marked emphasis on numbers in Jain mythology. Forbidden most occupations by their religion, they dealt in precious metals and stones and many became very wealthy. Jains wear white and take great care to avoid killing any living thing.

K Kajula Kadphises, one of 5 chieftains among whom Bactria was divided, founded the Kushan dynasty. This extended from northern India into central

Asia. He is known only from Chinese records.

Kalinga was conquered by ASOKA. In Asoka's own words, '150,000 were taken, 100,000 were killed, many more died'. Asoka went on to say that if one-thousandth part of the sufferings of Kalinga were to happen again, it would be 'pitiful and grievous' to him.

Kautilya, Chandragupta's brilliant minister, wrote the *Arthasastra* ('Manual of Politics') which advised how a king should keep his power. In order to do so Kautilya justified the use of kindness,

cruelty, justice, injustice, or any other means. Some scholars think that the Italian political philosopher Machiavelli (lived about AD

Buddhist monastery, Pakistan

eastern Asia, where they planted their Hindu-Buddhist culture which still survives in Thailand, Cambodia and Indonesia (especially Bali).

Aryan peoples from central Asia advanced through the mountain passes of the Himalaya into north-western India about 1500 BC, where they may have destroyed the Indus Valley civilization. They found India inhabited by darker-skinned Dravidians who they conquered or pushed southwards. Little is known about the next 1200 years.

The Macedonians and the Mauryas

Alexander the Great conquered Persia and then occupied the Indus Valley region briefly in 326–325 BC. The departure of the last Macedonian governor a few years later, left a power vacuum. Into this gap stepped Chandragupta Maurya, a low-caste adventurer who is said to have once gained Alexander's favour. Chandragupta quickly occupied northern India eastwards to Pataliputra and southwards to the Narbada River. In 305 BC he defeated another invasion

Left: A capital from one of Asoka's pillars carries the lion that now symbolizes India. Asoka, a conqueror who renounced war, had the Buddhist principles of his rule engraved on 25 pillars and rocks throughout his Indian empire.

Right: The Shwe Dagon, Burma's ancient pagoda, was first constructed shortly after Indian missionaries took Buddhism to the country more than 2,000 years ago. Its massive conical stupa, which devotees have plated thick with gold, rises nearly 100 metres above the main temple platform. Some 64 smaller stupas surround it. Thousands of precious stones stud its topmost *hti* (umbrella).

by a large force of Macedonians.

The Aryan-Dravidian religion of Hinduism was increasingly challenged by Jainism and Buddhism. Chandragupta became a Jain. His son, BINDUSARA, extended the Maurya kingdom southwards. About 272 BC, Chandragupta's grandson Asoka became king. In conquering the state of KALINGA (eastern India) Asoka caused the death of 250,000 Kalingans. In remorse, he renounced aggressive war, turned Buddhist, and encouraged the spread of Buddhism throughout the Indian subcontinent. Until Asoka died in 232 BC, India enjoyed a golden age of Buddhist rule, but about 183 BC, an army general called PUSYAMITRA SUNGA seized power from the last Maurya king and tried to restore Hinduism.

Mongol rule over northern India

The armies of Han China continued their pressure on the HSIUNG NU *(see page 57)* who in turn threatened another Mongol people, the YUEH-CHIH. These nomads pushed the Scythian Sakas through the Greek-occupied, ex-Persian satrapy of Bactria, into the PUNJAB. The Sakas ruled the Punjab from about 80 BC. The Yueh-chih pushed on. About AD 80 a Yueh-chih chieftain, KUJULA KADPHISES, became ruler of a kingdom that extended from central Asia into northern India. This was known as the KUSHAN KINGDOM. Buddhism was taken from Kushan by Yueh-chih missionaries into China. Little is known about the Kushan kingdom, or about the history of India during the following 200 years.

1500) modelled his book *The Prince* on Kautilya's book.
Kushan kingdom, established by KAJULA KADPHISES in AD 76 or later, lasted 200 years.

L Literature of ancient India was vast. The sacred *Vedas* included the *Brahmanas, Upanishads,* and the 2 epics: MAHABHARATA and RAMAYANA. Buddhist works (in the Pali language) included *Tripitaka* ('Three Baskets') and the *Suttas* ('Sermons') which contained the highly readable *Jataka Tales.*

M Mahabharata tells of a colossal war fought between 2 royal families. Gods and heroes took sides. The war probably symbolized

Stone elephant, Delhi

the Aryan–Dravidian struggle.
Mathura was the centre of a style of art rivalling Gandhara. It dated from about AD 100 and was Buddhist–Jain. It showed less Greco-Roman influence than the Gandhara style.
Meat eating was normal in Chandragupta's India, although higher castes did not eat the meat of horned cattle. Asoka encouraged vegetarianism. By AD 400 higher castes had given up meat.

O Outcastes were divided into 2 groups:

Hindus who had no caste, and non-Hindus, such as Jains, Buddhists and foreigners. Outcastes (probably descended from enslaved prisoners-of-war) were until recently treated badly.

P Punjab was ruled by the Sakas, a Scythian dynasty, from about 80 BC to AD 388.
Pusyamitra Sunga, a brahmin general of the last Maurya king, usurped the throne.

R Ramayana is a wealth of legends, myths and

historical facts woven into a fascinating epic. The story concerns Rama (a dispossessed prince) and the abduction of his wife Sita.

S Stupas were huge dome-shaped burial mounds built to hold relics of the Buddha and saints. They were the forerunners of Sri Lankan dagobas and Chinese, Japanese and Burmese pagodas.

Y Yueh-chih were Indo-Scythians who ruled Bactria and part of northern India about 128 BC – AD 450.

Index

Lao Tzu, Taoism and, **59**
Larsa, *11*, **12**
Lascaux Caves painting, *8*
Law,
  Babylonian, **37**
Lebanon, Cedars of, **40–1**
Legalist philosophy, **59**
Leisure,
  Indus Valley, *24*
  Stone Age, **9**
  Sumerian, *15*
Lettuces, **36**
Levant, **21**
Levers, **9**
Library,
  Ashurbanipal's, **46**
Libyans, **21**
Linear A/B, *27*, **30**, *30*
Literature,
  Chinese (Taoist), **59**, **60**
  Egyptian, **17**, *17*, **23**
  Hebrew, *53–4*, *54*
  Homeric, **29**
  Indian, **63**, **64**
  Sumerian, **14**, *14*
Liu Hsiu, **58**
Liu Pang, **58**
Lower Egypt, **21**

M
Macedonia(ns), **21**
  Timechart, *4–5*
Magi, **50**, *50*
  Gaumata and, **50**
Mahabharata, **64**
Mali,
  Timechart, *5*
Mallia, *29*, **30**
Manasa, **63**
Mandarins, **59**
Marathon, *49*, **50**
Marduk, **35**, **36**
Mari, *33*
Mathematics,
  Egyptian, **21**
Mathura, **64**
Maurya(ns), *62*
  Map, *61*
  Timechart, *5*
Maya,
  Timechart, *5*
Media, *44*, **46**
Memphis, *16*, **22**
Menkare's pyramid, *17*
Mercenaries, **41**
Mes-kalam-du, King, *14*
Mesopotamia, **12**
Messiah, **53**, **54**
Migration,
  Primitive man, **9**
Miletus, *27*
Ming dynasty,
  Timechart, *5*
Minoans, *see* Aegean Peoples
Minos, **30**
Mitanni, **39**
Mithras, **50**, **51**
Moabites, **54**
Mohenjo daro, *24*, **25**
  Great Bath at, *25*
Money,
  Chinese, **56**
  Persian, **50**, **51**
Mongols,
  Drama, **59**
  Hsiung Nu and, **56**, **57**
  Timechart, *4–5*
Moses, **54**
Mughals,
  Timechart, *5*
Mummies, **22**, *22*
Mursilis I, **36**
Mutwatallis, **39**
Mycale, *49*, **51**
Mycenae, *29*, **30–1**, **30**, *31*
  in Timechart, *5*
Myrrh, Frankincense and, **50**
Myths/Mythology,
  Atlantis, **27**, **28**
  Babylonian, *34*, **35**
  Egyptian, **21**
  Europa, **28**
  Hittite, **39**
  Indian, *62–3*, **63**
  Mycenaean, **32**
  Sumerian, **13**

N
Nabonidus, **36**
Nabopolassar, **37**
Nabu-nasir, **37**
Nakht, Tomb of, *17*
Nanna, **13**
Naram-Sin, **13**
  Stele, *14*
Neanderthal man, **10**
Nebuchadnezzar II, **37**, *37*
Necho, **37**
Nehemiah, **55**
Nepthys, **21**
Nile, fishing on, *19*
Nilometers, **22**, *22*
Nimrud, *44*, **47**
  Mona Lisa of, *42*
Nin-gal, **13**
Nineveh, *44*, **47**
Nippur, *11*, **13**

Normans,
  Timechart, *5*

O
Obelisk, *21*
Odysseus,
  Odyssey and, **30**
Olmecs,
  Timechart, *5*
Ormuzd, *see* Ahura-Mazda
Osiris, *21*, **22**
Outcastes, **64**

P
Palestine, **37**, **41**
Paper, **59**
Parthians, **51**
Parvati, *63*
Peloponnesus, *29*, **30**
Persepolis, *49*, **51**, **51**, *52*
Persian Gulf, **13**
Persians, **49–52**, *51*
  Agriculture, **51**
  Art(s), **49–50**
  Architecture, *51–2*
  Dynasties, **49**
  Government, **49**
  Language, **51**
  Map, *49*
  Money, **50**, **51**
  Religion, **50**
  Timechart, *4–5*
Phaestos, *29*, **31**, *31*
Pharaoh, **22**
Philistines, **42**
Philosophy,
  Chinese, **59**
Phoenicians, **40–3**, *42*
  Alphabet, **40**
  Carthage and, **43**
  Dyes, **41**, *42*
  Glass, **41**, *43*
  Ivory work, **40**, *43*
  Map, *40*
  Religion, **42**, *42*
  Sacrifice, **42**
  Seafarers, **41**
  Ships, **40–1**, *43*
  Timechart, *4–5*
  Trade, **40–1**, *41*
Pictographs, *13*, *15*
  Chinese, *57*
  Indus Valley, **25**, *26*
  Seals and, **14**
Pilate, **55**
Poseidon, **31**
Printing matrix, clay, *34*
Promised land, *53*
Prophets, **53**, **55**
Ptah, *21*
Ptolemies,
  Timechart, *5*
Pu-Abi, Queen, **11**, **13**, *13*
Punic Wars, **42**
  Carthage and, **43**
Punishment,
  Early man, **10**
Punjab, *61*, **64**
Pusyamitra Sunga, **64**, *64*
Pylos, *29*, **31**
Pyramids, **16–17**, *16–17*, **23**

Q
Queen Pu-Abi,
  Burial ceremony, **13**
  Burial chamber of, **11**
  Grave objects, *13*

R
Ra, *20*, **22**, *42*
Races, **10**
Rajasthan, **25**
Ramapithecus, **6**
Ramayana, *63*, **64**
Ramses II, *21*, **22**
Red,
  Eyebrows, **60**
Reliefs, Assyrian, *44-5*, *48*
Religion,
  Babylonian, **35**
  Buddhism, **61**, *61*, *62-3*
  Chinese, **59**
  Christian, **53**
  Early man, **8–9**
  Egyptian, **21**
  Hebrew, **53**, **55**
  Indian, **61**, *61*, **63**
  Persian, **50**
  Phoenician, **42**, *42*
Rhodes, **31**
Rice farming, *57*
Ritual bathing, **25**
Roads,
  Assyrian, **47**
Romans,
  Timechart, *5*
Rome, **42**
  Punic Wars and, **42**
Rosetta Stone, *19*, **22**
Royal road, Persian, *49*, *49*

S
Sacae, **51**
Sacrifice,
  Phoenician, **42**
Salamis, *49*, **51**
Samos, *49*

Santorina, *27*, **30**
Saqqara, *16*, **22**, *23*
Sardis, *49*, **52**
Sargon II, **47**, *47*, **48**
Sargon of Akkad, *11*, **15**
  Seal, **14**, *14*
Sassanians,
  Timechart, *5*
Satrapies, *49*, **52**
Saul, **55**
Saxons,
  Timechart, *5*
Schliemann,
  Heinrich, **31**
  Sophie, *31*
  Troy and, **32**
Science,
  Babylonian, **35**, **37**
  Chinese, **59**
Script, pictographic, **25**
Scythians, **39**
Seals, cylinder,
  Babylonian, *35-6*
  Indus Valley, **26**
  Sumerian, **14**, *14-5*
Seleucids,
  Timechart, *5*
Semites, **14**
Sennacherib, **45**, **47**, **48**
Seth, *20*, **22**
Shaduf, *18*
Shang dynasty, **56**, **59**
  Timechart, *5*
Shatt-al-Arab, **14**
Shekel, **37**, *42*
Ships,
  Phoenician, **40–1**, *43*
Shwe Dagon pagoda, *64*
Sicily, **43**
Sidon, **40**, *43*
Siege, Assyrian, *46-7*
Silk route, *57*
Siva, **26**, *63*
Snake goddess, *30*
Sobek, *21*
Society,
  Babylonian, **33**, **37**
  Early man, **8–10**
  Indian, *61*, **61**
Soldier,
  Hittite, **39**
Solomon, **55**
Songhai,
  Timechart, *5*
South-East Asians, *see* Indians
Spain, **43**
Spaniards,
  in Timechart, *5*
Sparta, **52**
Spear-throwers, **10**
Spices, **31**
Sphinx, *17*, *21*
Standard of Ur, *11*, **14**, *14*
Stone Age, *see* Early man
Stonehenge, *10*
Stupas, *63*, **64**
Sudras, **61**
Sui dynasty,
  Timechart, *5*
Sumerians, **11-15**
  Agriculture, **15**
  Armour, **14**
  Art, *12*, **14**, **14**, *15*
  Gods, *11*, **12-13**
  Literature, **14**, **14**
  Map, *11*
  Seals, **14**, *14-15*
  Timechart, *4–5*
  Toy, *15*
  Writing, **13**, *15*
Sung dynasty,
  Timechart, *5*
Surveying,
  Egyptian, *19*
Susa, *49*, **51**, **52**
Syria, **37**

T
Talanton, **31**
Talmud, **54**
Tang dynasty,
  Timechart, *5*
Tanit, **40**
Taoism, **59**, *59*, *60*
Taxes,
  Assyrian, **45**, **48**
  Persian, **50**
Technology,
  Early man, **6-8**, *10*
Ten commandments, **55**
Thebes,
  in Egypt, *16*, **20**, **22-3**
Thermopylae, **52**
Theseus, **31**
Thoth, *20*, **23**
Thrace, *49*, **52**, **80**
Thracians, **32**
Tiamat, **37**
Tiglath-Pileser III, **48**
Tigris, **15**
Tikal, *120*, *121*
  Timechart, *4-5*
Tiryns, *27*, **32**
Toltecs,
  Timechart, *5*
Tombstone, Punic, *43*
Torah, **53**

Tower of Babel, **37**
Town planning,
  Indus Valley people, **25**
Trade,
  Chinese, **57**
  Egyptian, **18**
  Indian, **62**
  Indus Valley, **25**
  Phoenician, **40–1**, *41*
Tribes,
  Early man, **8-9**
Tribute, **48**, **50**, *52*
Trojan War, **32**, *32*
Troy, *27*, **32**
  Schliemann and, **31**
Tutankhamun, **20-1**, **23**, *23*
Tyre, **40**, **43**
Tyrian purple, **41**, *42*

U
Upper Egypt, **23**
Ur, *11*, **12**, **15**
  City plan, *12*
  Housing, *12*
  Standard of, *11*, **14**, *14*
  Ziggurat, *13*
Utnapishtim, **14**

V
Vaisyas, **61**
Valley of the Kings, **23**
Varaha, *62*
Venus of Willendorf, *9*
Vikings,
  Timechart, *4-5*
Vishnu, *62*
  Follower, *61*

W
Wall,
  Carthage, **43**
Warfare,
  Assyrian, **44-5**, *46-7*
Warring States period, **60**
Weapons,
  Assyrian chariots, **45**, *44-8*
  Early man, **10**
  Hittite, **38-9**
  Minoan/Mycenean, **30**, **32**
  Persian, **51**
  Sumerian, **14**
Weights and measures, in Indus
  Valley, **26**, *26*
Wheat, emmer, **39**
Wheeled vehicles, **15**, *15*
  See also Chariots
Winged bulls, **48**, *48*
Witch doctors, *9*
Wu, Emperor, **58**, **60**

X
Xerxes I, **52**, *52*

Y
Yahweh (God), **53**
  Moses and, **54**
Yellow turbans, **60**
Yin-chu, *56*, **60**
Yueh-chih, **64**, *64*

Z
Zagros Mountains, *11*
Zapotecs,
  Timechart, *5*
Zeus, **32**, *32*
Ziggurat,
  Tower of Babel, **35**, **37**
  Ur, *13*, **15**
Zoroaster/Zoroastrians, **50**, *52*
Zoser, King, *16*, **22**, *23*

Acknowledgements

Contributing artists
Marion Appleton, Peter Archer, Charles Bannerman, Raymond
Brown, Richard Coggan, Chris Forsey, Geoff Hunt, Ivan Lapper,
Dennis Lascelles, Jim Marks, Nigel Osborne

The Publishers also wish to thank the following:
Aerofilms 10B
Jean Bottin 33C, 43B
British Museum 18-19T, 44C, 45C
J. Allan Cash 18TC
Peter Clayton 19C, 22B, 23BL, 28BR, 30CR B, 31BL BR, 42, 49BR
Colorpix 7B, 18BR, 20BR, 21BL BR, 57TR, 62TL, 63TR, 64TR
Werner Forman Archive 35B, 38BC BR, 40BC, 41BL, 42B, 44BL, 45B, 49BC, 50C, 57BC, 59BR, 60BC
Richard & Sally Greenhill 57C
Sonia Halliday 31C, 32C, 53CL
Robert Harding Associates 6B, 8B, 9B, 29B, 33BC, 34T, 44BL, 46B, 47BC BR, 48B, 50BR, 51BC, 52T,
56B C, 57BR, 58BC BR, 59CR BC, 60CL BR
Michael Holford 7TR, 9TL, 14TR, 15TR, 17TL TR, 19TR, 36TL TR, 37T, 45TR, 47TR, 48CL, 54B, 59TR,
64BL
William Macquitty 21TR, 25TR CR B, 50BL, 51BR, 52B, 54TL, 61CL
Mansell Collection 12TR, 18BL
Musée du Louvre/Hubert Josse 43TL
Musées Nationaux, Paris 14TL
Josephine Powell 24T, 26B, 28T, 30CR, 31T, 32T, 61BC BR, 62BC BR, 63BC BR, 64B
Ronald Sheridan 9TR, 11CR B, 12C B, 13C TR B, 14C B, 15TL BL B TC, 16B, 17BC BR, 19TL C B, 20R
BL, 21TC, 27B, 28BC, 32B, 33BR, 34BC BR, 36B, 37B, 39B, 40TR BR, 41BR, 43CL, 48TR, 50TL TR, 53B,
55TR B BR
Snark International 11CL, 36CR, 51TR
Ziolo/R. Roland 26C